The Circle Line

including the Hammersmith & City Line

Desmond F. Croome

GW00482940

Capital Transport

First published 2003

ISBN 185414 267 4

Published in association with London's Transport Museum
by Capital Transport Publishing, 38 Long Elmes, Harrow Weald, Middlesex

Printed by CS Graphics, Singapore

© Desmond F. Croome 2003

The author and the publisher would like to thank Mike Horne for substantial assistance in the preparation of this book. The cover painting is by Peter Green GRA.

CONTENTS

The name Circle Line did not appear on the Underground map until 1949, having made an appearance as a line distinguished from the Metropolitan and District lines two years earlier, when the term Inner Circle was still being used. An early reference to 'Circle Line' is shown in this poster diagram of 1936. LT Museum

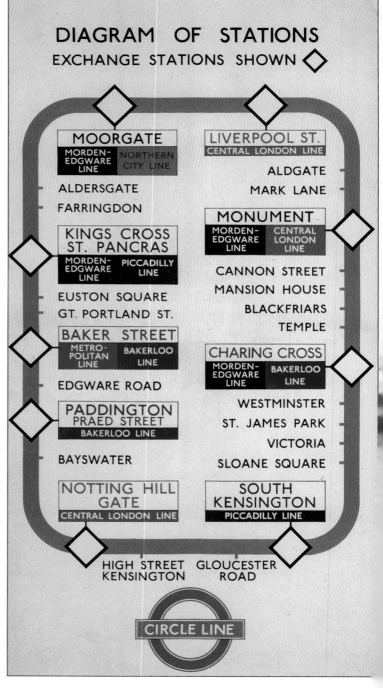

DIAGRAM OF STATIONS
EXCHANGE STATIONS SHOWN ◇

MOORGATE
MORDEN-EDGWARE LINE — NORTHERN CITY LINE

ALDERSGATE
FARRINGDON

KINGS CROSS ST. PANCRAS
MORDEN-EDGWARE LINE — PICCADILLY LINE

EUSTON SQUARE
GT. PORTLAND ST.

BAKER STREET
METRO-POLITAN LINE — BAKERLOO LINE

EDGWARE ROAD

PADDINGTON PRAED STREET
BAKERLOO LINE

BAYSWATER

NOTTING HILL GATE
CENTRAL LONDON LINE

LIVERPOOL ST.
CENTRAL LONDON LINE

ALDGATE
MARK LANE

MONUMENT
MORDEN-EDGWARE LINE — CENTRAL LONDON LINE

CANNON STREET
MANSION HOUSE
BLACKFRIARS
TEMPLE

CHARING CROSS
MORDEN-EDGWARE LINE — BAKERLOO LINE

WESTMINSTER
ST. JAMES PARK
VICTORIA
SLOANE SQUARE

SOUTH KENSINGTON
PICCADILLY LINE

HIGH STREET KENSINGTON   GLOUCESTER ROAD

CIRCLE LINE

Early Days

London Underground's Circle Line is, as Italy was described in 1847, little more than a geographical expression. Unlike the other Underground lines, it has no single company as ancestor, it owned no track, rolling stock or stations, but for many years had to rely on the District and Metropolitan Railways for its locomotives and carriages, track and stations. The story of the Circle Line is bound up with the arrival of the main line railways in London, and the need to provide connections between them. The Hammersmith & City Line is nearly as ethereal, the services for many years being run as a part of the Metropolitan Line; only comparatively recently has official status been granted to a name used descriptively by its regular customers and staff for at least a half century. Furthermore the eastern end of the Hammersmith & City operates over tracks shared with the District Line and the detailed history of that section fits more naturally with the history of the District Line, to which readers are referred.

The first main line railways established London termini at London Bridge (1836), Euston (1837), Paddington (1838), Shoreditch (1840) and Fenchurch Street (1841). There were many railway promotions in 1844–1847, rising to a crescendo in the 1846 Session, when the Commons considered 435 railway bills for England and Wales. In that year the Government established a Royal Commission on London Termini, but rather prejudiced the outcome by itself defining a central railway-free zone (bounded by the present Pentonville Road, City Road, Finsbury Square, Bishopsgate, London Bridge, Borough High Street and Road, Lambeth Road, Vauxhall Bridge (and Bridge Road), Grosvenor Place, Park Lane, Edgware Road, then via the present Circle Line alignment via Marylebone Road and Euston Road back to King's Cross). The Commission's main task was to specify which new railways should be allowed to penetrate this zone. The answer was 'none', except for the Nine Elms–Waterloo extension already authorised. This ruling was not an absolute embargo but a strong recommendation to Select Committees of the Commons or Lords considering future railway bills.

So the pattern was established of holding back the London termini at an invisible ring-wall. However, even if the Royal Commission had not existed, extensions to the very centre of London (which was much smaller then) were also discouraged by the high costs of acquiring land and demolishing property, and by the actions taken by the landed aristocracy to preserve the integrity of their central London estates.

With surface railways effectively barred from most of central London, thoughts turned to building railways underground. There were physical and legal problems in tunnelling beneath buildings. Legally, if a tunnel were planned to run beneath any part of a building, the railway promoters were obliged, in the absence of any agreement, to buy the whole building. Physically, much skilled work was involved in shoring up and underpinning buildings so that they did not disintegrate or slide into the excavation. Newly-built public roads offered a partial solution to these problems; two roads, in particular, played a fundamental role in determining the alignment of the future Circle. One was the so-called New Road, built across open country in 1756 from Paddington at Edgware Road to Islington at the Angel intersection. By 1857 the name 'New' had lost its significance, and it was renamed, from the west, Marylebone Road, Euston Road and Pentonville Road.

Further south, the Corporation of the City of London pursued a slow moving scheme to create the present Farringdon Street. In 1838 it obtained powers to extend the new road northwards to Clerkenwell Green. Here in the Fleet Valley was a need, not merely for a new road, but a comprehensive scheme to remove slums and cover the partly-open Fleet Sewer. Charles Pearson, the City Solicitor, devoted a great deal of his time and money to advocating a group of central terminal stations on either side of Farringdon Street south of the present Holborn Viaduct, with a further 14 acres area north of the viaduct for local passenger trains, goods depots and an engine shed. In a covered way beneath a 100ft-wide road, the six standard-gauge and two broad-gauge tracks would have connected with the Great Northern Railway at King's Cross and the Great Western at Paddington. However, the expected financial support from the City of London and the main line railways was not forthcoming, so Pearson and some associates deposited a City Terminus Bill in the 1852/3 session of Parliament. At the same time a separate group of promoters proposed an underground line following the New Road from Paddington (Sussex Gardens at Westbourne Terrace) to King's Cross, where it would join the City Terminus Railway and so provide a through route from Paddington to Holborn Hill. To overcome local opposition the line was shortened by moving the western terminus to east of Edgware Road.

This latter scheme gained Royal Assent on 15th August 1853, under the name of the North Metropolitan Railway. Pearson's City Terminus Bill was not supported by the City Corporation, and failed at an early stage. The North Metropolitan group still needed access to the City, and the Great Western Railway also took an interest. A modified scheme was evolved, which abandoned the large Farringdon Street terminus and turned eastwards to the General Post Office at St Martins-le-Grand. In the west, the proposed line was extended from Edgware Road to Praed Street opposite Paddington station, with a spur to the east side of the Great Western terminus. There were also spurs to the Great Northern at King's Cross and the London and North Western at Euston. The scheme received Royal Assent on 7th August 1854, repealing the powers of the previous scheme and taking the name 'Metropolitan Railway'.

Although parliamentary powers had been won, perhaps the most difficult task lay ahead – that of raising capital. This was especially daunting for a scheme exploiting the entirely new concept of travelling underground. By 1856 the City Corporation had at last completed its new street from Holborn Hill to Clerkenwell Green (the present Farringdon Road) and had cleared the land on each side, following the removal of Smithfield cattle market to a site north of King's Cross. This presented an unrepeatable opportunity to buy land in the Fleet Valley at a reasonable price. However, the only firm promise of financial support was a limited amount from the Great Western. In order to concentrate the minds of other authorities which supported the scheme in principle, a winding-up bill was prepared for the 1857/8 session, and deposited. However, the money markets improved, the Metropolitan's board was strengthened by two new able and competent directors, and, following strong pressure from Charles Pearson, the City Corporation agreed to buy £200,000 of shares as soon as the rest of the capital was properly subscribed. The Farringdon Street to General Post Office section was abandoned, and the short section into the proposed Metropolitan Praed Street station was postponed. These alterations were sanctioned by an Act of 8th August 1859, and sufficient capital was raised to begin construction.

Constructing what became the Circle Line was very disruptive. This view in Craven Hill shows the inconvenience caused to road users and frontagers. LT Museum

In December 1859, civil engineering contracts were awarded to John Jay for the Farringdon – Euston Square section, and to Smith and Knight for Euston Square – Paddington. The contractors were instructed to start the works in March 1860, but some sinking of shafts began in February. The City Corporation duly invested its £200,000 in August 1860.

The main Metropolitan began at a new Bishop's Road station at Paddington, then continued past its future junction with the Circle Line (Praed Street junction), and proceeded eastwards with intermediate stations at Edgware Road, Baker Street, Portland Road (now Great Portland Street), Gower Street (now Euston Square), King's Cross, to end at a temporary Farringdon Street station, on the north side of the present Cowcross Street at its junction with Farringdon Road.

The western section of the new line was principally beneath the New Road, and construction was simpler than for the eastern section. Here, the works were mainly of the cut-and-cover type. This involved closing a whole section of street, digging a trench 33ft 6in wide, with the sides temporarily supported by timber shoring, then constructing brick side walls 28ft 6in apart, three bricks thick with a rise of 11ft. There was normally no masonry or concrete to form an 'invert' between the two side walls, and these walls had no concrete foundations beneath the 6ft wide footings. On top of the side walls there was an elliptical arch of rings of bricks, the number of rings varying from five to eight, depending on the estimated final loading. In places where there was insufficient depth for an arch, cast iron cross-girders were used instead, spaced from 6ft to 8ft apart. Between King's Cross and Farringdon, the contractor had to build the 728-yard Clerkenwell Tunnel, but otherwise this section was mainly in open cutting. Provision had to be made for the line to cross the Fleet Sewer three times, and much of the excavation was through an old dump of dust and debris.

There was no precedent for some of the Metropolitan's civil engineering problems, such as diverting sewers and pipes and ensuring that the many adjacent buildings survived undamaged. Part of the unfinished cutting, near Tunbridge Place, New Road, collapsed on 24th May 1861, bringing down gas and water mains, telegraph wires, pavements and gardens. The damage was mostly repaired within a week, but on 18th June 1862, after a torrential storm, the Fleet Sewer broke into the works in Farringdon Road and filled them with dirty water. This was mostly repaired by 6th August 1862.

The right-of-way for the main line between Paddington and Farringdon was equipped with three rails in each direction to allow the operation of both standard gauge (4ft 8½ ins) and broad gauge (7ft 0¼ in) rolling stock, with the common rail being adjacent to the station platforms. The track itself consisted of iron running rails, weighing 62-lb per yard, of flat-bottomed section, bolted to longitudinal sleepers. A $\frac{1}{16}$ in layer of steel at the top of each rail was intended to reduce the rate of wear, but it disintegrated under traffic and by 1866 the whole line had been relaid with steel 86-lb flat-bottomed rails and transverse sleepers. From 1873 this was replaced by standard British chaired bull-head rail. At King's Cross connections were made to the Great Northern Railway, joining the main line just to the north of the train shed.

Platform view of typical station during construction. LT Museum

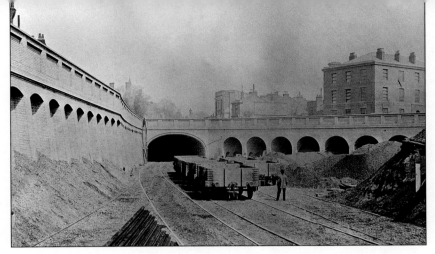

View of construction works just east of Edgware Road station looking towards Baker Street. The railway's repair facilities are yet to be built on the right side. LT Museum

John Fowler (1817–1898; knighted 1885, baronet 1890) was appointed engineer of the Metropolitan in 1853, and continued throughout the construction period. He overcame the civil engineering problems with brilliant success, but was less successful in his attempt to provide a locomotive which did not emit smoke or fumes in the tunnels (experimental fireless locomotives were built and tested but were found impracticable). In the end the GWR ordered twenty-two 38-ton 2-4-0 well tanks, with a facility to divert exhaust steam into the cold water tanks, under control of the driver. When this diversion was made, it prevented the emission of steam and stopped the draught which otherwise kept the fire burning brightly. However, it could not entirely stop the discharge of foul vapours from the burning coke, the Metropolitan's infrastructure having been built on the assumption that fireless type locomotives would be used. Twelve locomotives were delivered in time for the opening and by October 1864, a further ten had been received.

The 42ft coaches supplied by the Great Western had eight wheels in a rigid arrangement, with special linkages to negotiate curves. Thirty-nine coaches were built new and six were rebuilt from existing GW stock. A complete train provided first, second and third class seating.

The signalling system caused some problems, and the Government inspectors had some reservations in granting their approval. At first the railway favoured a mechanical system, with a signal at the departure end of each platform with two arms on a common pivot. One was worked by the signalman at that station (i.e. the starting signal) and the other (by a connecting solid iron wire) by the signalman at the next station beyond (i.e. the home signal of that signalbox). The starting signal could not be lowered until the home signal has been lowered, and the driver could not start until both signals were clear. This was soon replaced by an early electric system devised by C.E. Spagnoletti, the Great Western's telegraph engineer. This consisted essentially of an electric circuit controlled by the signalman at the station beyond. When a train had left his station, he depressed and locked a key to send an electric current to the signalbox in rear, which showed 'line clear' on a flag inside a telegraph instrument. If no current was flowing, the indication 'Train on Line' appeared instead. The signalmen also had a simple bell code system to offer trains forward.

Portland Road station towards the end of the nineteenth century.

The style of the station street elevations has been described as 'debased Italianate', based on imitation stonework and mouldings of concrete rendering. However, it did have the merit of adopting a consistent general style for the whole line. Layouts varied greatly depending on the topography of the line at each location, but each station had to provide an entrance hall, booking office and various staff rooms. Baker Street and Gower Street (Euston Square) were almost entirely below ground. At street level the only buildings were small pavilions on each side of the road, with separate booking offices for the up and down lines. Space was found for the platforms by extra-wide excavations for the retaining walls (45ft). The arches of the retaining walls were carried outward and upward to form skylights emerging in the front gardens of houses. Portland Road was similar, but without the skylights; as the alignment of the tracks left the road for a short distance to cut across a curve, the station entrance could spread itself across an island, so that a ticket office could be built across the line. The single-storey entrance was flanked by two small cylindrical structures capped by domes, but these were removed in 1869–70 to improve ventilation.

King's Cross and Edgware Road were in open cutting, with high arched roofs of wrought iron and glass, supported on arcaded retaining walls. The booking office buildings were across the line at Edgware Road and parallel to the line at King's Cross, adjoining the upper extensions of the retaining walls, one for each direction. Farringdon Street, in a cutting, had a temporary wooden booking office across the lines, as there was a firm proposal to extend to Moorgate, known before station construction began. The Bishops Road ticket office was a large single-storey structure with a forecourt for cabs and buses. The platforms were in a cutting between arcaded brick retaining walls, protected from the weather by a bow girder and plate glass roof. Edgware Road station, in fact in Burne Street (a side street further east), was unique in being dressed in artificial stone.

Stations were lit by coal-gas lamps in large glass globes, suspended above the platforms, but extra gas lights were added in 1864, along the rear walls of the platforms.

It had been hoped to open the new railway in time for the International Exhibition of 1862, but mishaps and unforeseen complications caused slippage in completion. Some trial trips were made on completed sections on 28th November 1861, and there was a trial run throughout the line on 24th May 1862. On 30th August 1862 further full-length trials were made, with the Government Inspector of Railways being conveyed in the morning and the shareholders in the afternoon. A second Board of Trade inspection took place on 22nd December 1862, but some signalling alterations were required, and two final official inspections were made on 30th December 1862 and 3rd January 1863. Then followed daily trial running from 4th to 8th January, and the official opening ceremony on 9th January. Two special trains, together carrying about 600 directors, shareholders and others connected with the company left Bishops Road soon after 13.00 and stopped intermediately for the guests to inspect Edgware Road, Baker Street, Portland Road and King's Cross. The trains arrived at Farringdon Street at about 15.10, and the occupants sat down to a rather unsuitably-timed banquet, where the usual self congratulatory speeches were delivered, not forgetting the efforts of Charles Pearson, who had died on 14th September 1862.

Cutting the way outside Paddington station, circa 1866.
LT Museum

Inner Circle train approaching Aldgate on an 'outer rail' working. LT Museum

Public service began on Saturday 10th January 1863, and passengers swarmed in to sample the new experience, despite there being only a basic 15-minute service. Public apprehension about the adverse effects of underground trains on buildings was reflected in a 'Punch' poem:

> I thunder down to work each morn
> And some historic shrine
> Must have its matchless fabric torn
> To get me there at nine
> And when I gather up my traps
> As sundown sets me free
> A nation's monuments collapse
> To take me home to tea.

After the initial flurry of passengers making a trial journey, traffic stabilised at an encouragingly high level, and by 30th June 1863, roundly 4.8 million passengers had been carried. The Metropolitan proprietors had to learn the hard way that the foremost quality that the public demanded of a rapid transit railway was reliability, and that this was best achieved on a short, simple line with few junctions. At first the policy could be expressed as 'let 'em all come', with other companies' passenger and goods trains being welcomed to use the Metropolitan's tracks and so contribute to its revenue. The clash between the needs of local and through passengers sowed the seeds of the initial dispute with the Great Western. The Metropolitan had wanted a 10-minute service between 08.00 and 20.00, but by April 1863 the GWR could do no more than give this service in peak hours, with a 15-minute service between the peaks. The GWR sought to protect its own future through services. The junctions at King's Cross between the Metropolitan and Great Northern were the last straw, and their physical completion in

July 1863 caused the Great Western to give notice to withdraw all locomotives and carriages after traffic on 30th September, later amended to 10th August. The Great Northern Railway was anxious to secure the continued existence of the Metropolitan to safeguard access for its own trains to the City of London. It had already built some 'condensing' locomotives for its own future services, and hastily adapted other locomotives in its fleet to 'condense'. From 11th August the Paddington-Farringdon Street service was maintained by Great Northern locomotives and a mixture of Great Northern and London & North Western carriages. As the Great Western had used broad-gauge rolling stock, the third rail needed for standard gauge had hitherto been unused, and the newly discovered misalignments caused a few derailments, whilst the shortage of rolling stock compelled the peak service to be reduced to 15-minute intervals. However, practical politics obliged the Great Western and Metropolitan to make peace, and an agreement to tie up some loose ends was made in October 1863.

The Metropolitan had ordered its own rolling stock almost as soon as it opened, and asked the locomotive makers Beyer Peacock to supply 18 standard-gauge locomotives, also ordering 34 carriages from the Ashbury Railway Carriage and Iron Company. The locomotives were powerful machines of the 4-4-0T type, and were so satisfactory that, with relatively minor modifications, repeat orders were placed until the Metropolitan had acquired a fleet of 66 similar machines. The competing Metropolitan District Railway also bought 54 locomotives which were almost identical. The carriages were effectively narrow-gauge versions of the Great Western 'rigid eights', and included a variety of ingenious (but not wholly satisfactory) arrangements to allow them to negotiate curves. The initial delivery comprised 34 vehicles, but deliveries of new carriages of the same type continued until 1884, when the fleet numbered 301 vehicles. In an effort to find smaller and lighter carriages 26 close-coupled 4-wheel vehicles were delivered in 1869, although they were mostly employed on the St John's Wood line.

Locomotive and carriage shops at Chapel Street, east of Edgware Road station, were completed early in 1865 and looked after all the Metropolitan's rolling stock (these shops soon became quite inadequate and the Metropolitan opened replacement facilities near Neasden from 1882, for carriages, and 1883, for locomotives).

The connections at King's Cross, which had been one of the reasons for the disagreement with the Great Western, were used by through Great Northern suburban passenger trains from 1st October 1863, when they ran through to Farringdon Street. In the 'up' or eastbound direction, these trains had a separate platform at the north end of the York Road curve, which was named as 'King's Cross – York Road' and opened on 1st January 1866. A platform was opened at the northern end of the Hotel Curve on 1st February 1878, thereby giving the Great Northern through trains an intermediate platform in each direction.

With the expected pressure on line capacity caused by the through running of other companies' services, the Metropolitan board decided, early in 1863, to use powers obtained on 11th July 1861 to construct two extra tracks between King's Cross and Farringdon Street. Their continuation to Moorgate Street had been authorised by acts of 6th August 1861 and 25th July 1864. The works, under the name of the 'City Widened Lines' began soon after the Great Northern through services were temporarily suspended on 1st July 1867, and involved making new connections at King's Cross and the construction of a second Clerkenwell Tunnel, 733 yards long, which descended towards Farringdon Street so that, just south of the tunnel mouth, it burrowed beneath the original Metropolitan Line, which was carried over the Widened

Lines by a skew bridge known as the 'Ray Street gridiron'. The new lines then ascended at 1 in 40 to their platforms in Farringdon Street station, which now had two platforms for the Metropolitan and two for the Widened Lines. The extension used a resited Farringdon Street station, with four tracks sheltered by twin-arch elliptical wrought-iron roofs. The original Farringdon Street station closed after traffic on 28th February 1866.

At that time the City of London was the predominant source of employment, and was the objective of thousands of daily travellers. At Farringdon Street, the Metropolitan was on the fringe of the City, and parliamentary powers were obtained on 6th August 1861 for an extension to Moorgate Street. It opened on 23rd December 1865, with an intermediate station at Aldersgate Street (now Barbican). East of Farringdon Street, construction of the Widened Lines to Moorgate Street proceeded concurrently with that of the Circle or northern pair of tracks.

Through trains from the Great Western outer-suburban areas to the Metropolitan began on 1st October 1863, were suspended after 31st December 1863, and were resumed on 2nd May 1864. These trains were of broad gauge and were extended to Aldersgate Street on 1st March 1866 and to Moorgate Street on 1st July of the same year, using the Widened Lines from Farringdon which were equipped with the third rail for broad-gauge operation. The Hammersmith & City services were also extended to these stations on these dates, on the Metropolitan's tracks. The last broad gauge train ran on the Metropolitan on 14th March 1869, to be replaced by standard-gauge Great Western trains, which thenceforth normally used the Metropolitan's tracks. The Widened Lines were also connected with the Midland Railway's new London extension north of St Pancras. The Midland started a service between Bedford and Moorgate Street on 13th July 1869. The St Pancras terminus opened on 1st October 1869, but trains from an extended number of suburban stations, including those on the Tottenham & Hampstead Junction line, continued to use the Widened Lines.

Changes to the various connections with other railways at Kings Cross had an impact on the Metropolitan's station there. The track of the eastbound Widened Line had to use the site of an existing northern platform, and as it was impossible to move the northern retaining wall without destroying the overall single-arched roof, a new platform was built at the east end of the original station. In the westbound direction, the Widened Lines trains used the north face of an island platform whose south face was used by eastbound Metropolitan trains.

Further powers were obtained, in the special circumstances described later in this chapter, for an extension from Moorgate Street to Tower Hill, on 29th July 1864, but physical construction now proceeded more slowly. Eventually, an extension into the Great Eastern's new Liverpool Street terminus opened on 1st February 1875. As soon as the nearby Metropolitan station at Bishopsgate was available for traffic on 12th July 1875, all the Metropolitan trains were diverted there, and the Liverpool Street connection never used again except for isolated through excursion trains. The Aldgate extension encountered construction problems worse than those to Moorgate, but it eventually opened on 18th November 1876, with a shuttle service from Bishopsgate. Through services across Bishopsgate began on 4th December 1876.

It may also be mentioned that the first stage of what became the Metropolitan Extension line, the Metropolitan & St John's Wood Railway, opened between Baker Street and just beyond Swiss Cottage station on 13th April 1868. This line is outside the scope of the present work, except for its role in feeding extra trains on to the Baker Street to Moorgate section of the Circle. The line was always worked by the

Diagram of the Metropolitan Railway in relation to the Euston Road at its junction with Tottenham Court Road. The pipe cutting into the arch of the railway tunnel shows a proposal for a 'pneumatic dispatch tube' by which parcels would be conveyed across London. Immediately under this are the street drains.

Metropolitan and through running to Moorgate had begun concurrently with the public opening, but because of difficulty in working the Baker Street junction, ceased after 8th March 1869, not to be resumed until 1907 and for many years as a peak hour service only.

In west London an independent company, the Hammersmith & City Railway, had obtained powers on 22nd July 1861 to build a new line 2¼ miles long, and equipped with broad and standard gauge tracks. Branching from the Great Western at Green Lane (near the later Westbourne Park station) and continuing in a large arc to a terminus near the north side of Hammersmith Broadway. It followed the northern edge of the then built-up area, and initially had intermediate stations at Ladbroke Grove (then named Notting Hill) and Shepherd's Bush. A branch from near Latimer Road connected to the West London Railway, giving access to Kensington (Addison Road) station.

The promoters included John Fowler, civil engineer for the original Metropolitan line, and David Ogilvie, a director of the Great Western. Fowler was selected as engineer for the new line, and the company's board was strengthened by nominees from the GWR and Metropolitan including John Parson, who was appointed chairman, and became Metropolitan chairman from 1865 to 1872. However, after some legal proceedings about the purchase of land that would be required by the railway, Parson resigned from the Hammersmith & City board in February 1864.

Metropolitan train at Hammersmith station shortly after it opened. The early Metropolitan carriages had pronounced 'clerestories' which contained the gas required for the internal lighting system. LT Museum

Of the 2 miles 38 chains of the new line, about 3,000 yards ran on brick viaduct, with the rails about 20ft above ground level, The opening to traffic was delayed by signalling problems, but the main section opened on 13th June 1864, with a 30-minute service between Hammersmith and Farringdon Street, operated by the Great Western with broad-gauge stock. The 39-chain branch from Latimer Road junction to Uxbridge Road junction on the West London Railway opened on 1st July 1864, with the carriages for Addison Road being uncoupled from the Hammersmith trains at Latimer Road and taken on by a separate locomotive, the reverse arrangement applying in the opposite direction.

The Hammersmith & City had always been supported by the Great Western and Metropolitan Railways, but, by stages, their participation became more formal, until the line was vested jointly in both companies from 1st July 1867. After agreement between the two companies in late 1864, the Metropolitan took over the Hammersmith service on 1st April 1865 with standard-gauge stock. The Great Western continued to operate its broad-gauge half-hourly service to Addison Road. The City end of both services extended to Aldersgate Street and on to Moorgate Street. A further Great Western/Metropolitan agreement, of August 1868, saw the last broad gauge trains between Addison Road and Moorgate Street, running on 14th March 1869, and the broad-gauge rails were soon removed from the Hammersmith & City and Metropolitan. Because of rolling stock shortage, the replacement Great Western standard-gauge service did not begin until 1st June 1869.

Meanwhile a further complication had arisen in the shape of a new London & South

Western line between Kensington and Richmond on 1st January 1869, with a station at Hammersmith (Grove Road) on a curved brick viaduct. This new line branched off the West London line a short distance north of Addison Road, then swung round through about 180 degrees to dive beneath the Hammersmith & City line north of Hammersmith, then to curve at 90 degrees to the west (via Grove Road) on its way to Richmond. The construction of this line made it necessary to resite the Hammersmith & City's Hammersmith station, and a new station opened on Hammersmith Broadway on 1st December 1868. A running connection between the two lines, north of Hammersmith, opened on 1st June 1870, with an hourly Great Western service between Paddington and Richmond. However, this service was withdrawn after 31st October 1870, not to be replaced until 1st October 1877, when a Metropolitan service began between Aldgate and Richmond.

Apart from Hammersmith station, the City line's early years witnessed several physical improvements which helped the working of trains and brought in extra passengers. On the West London line, Uxbridge Road station opened on 1st November 1869, conveniently sited at the east end of Shepherd's Bush Green. Latimer Road, just north of the junction with the Addison Road line, opened on 16th December 1868, and Westbourne Park, near the Green Lane junction, on 1st February 1866, the structures being predominantly wood. The Great Western provided two extra tracks on the north side of the main line, between Green Lane junction and Paddington (Bishops Road); these came into use on 30th October 1871, concurrently with a new station at Royal Oak and resited a station at Westbourne Park (the latter opened two days later). The Board of Trade understandably objected to the Hammersmith & City trains making a flat crossing with the Great Western main line, and a flyunder came into use on 12th May 1878.

From south of the Thames, the London, Chatham & Dover Railway built a line across the river to Ludgate Hill, a permanent station there opening on 1st June 1865. The Chatham company then exercised its powers to build an extension beneath Snow Hill, which descended on a 1 in 39 gradient to join the Metropolitan at West Street junction, which was at the end of a 10-chain branch from the Circle Line just east of Farringdon Street station. From 3rd January some Great Northern suburban trains were extended to Ludgate Hill, and from 1st August 1866 a joint Great Northern/Chatham service ran between Herne Hill and New Barnet or Hatfield. The Chatham company pressed the Metropolitan to obtain powers to build an east-facing curve from the north end of the Snow Hill tunnel to Smithfield Junction. An agreement specified that the Chatham company should run 80 passenger trains into Moorgate Street each weekday. The service (from Victoria) began on 1st September 1871, but the stipulated total of 80 trains was not reached until 1st January 1872. After 1875, the number dwindled steadily. From 1st January 1866, some Chatham trains were extended to King's Cross, and Great Northern, and other trains were extended to Farringdon Street. Inter-running between the Midland and Chatham railways soon followed, so that by 1875 there were through services between Hendon or South Tottenham and Victoria. Now that the Great Northern, Great Western and Midland Railways had obtained direct access to the City of London, goods depots were built to allow goods to be unloaded into warehouses or delivered to their final destinations. Smithfield Market depot (owned by the Metropolitan but with sidings leased to the Great Western) opened on 3rd May 1869, to be followed by the Great Northern depot at Farringdon Street on 21st November 1874, and the Midland depot at Whitecross Street on 1st January 1878.

A Circle Complete

We must now retrace our footsteps a little to examine the circumstances which led to the completion of the Circle. The successful opening of the Paddington–Farringdon Street section led to a flood of bills for new railways in London, arousing great concern among property owners. Parliament adopted the time-honoured solution of delegating the problem to a committee to sort out. An 1863 committee of the House of Lords examined the general question of improving London's communications and proposed that the desired connection between the main line termini be achieved by extending the Metropolitan from Moorgate Street (eastwards) and Paddington (westwards) to link with a new line on the north side of the Thames to form a complete circle. In November 1863 John Fowler put flesh on these bones with proposals, under the general name of the 'Metropolitan District Railways', to extend the Metropolitan from Moorgate Street via Tower Hill and Cannon Street to Blackfriars, then under an authorised Thames Embankment to Westminster. This would be met end-on by a Metropolitan extension from Paddington to Notting Hill Gate and South Kensington.

In 1864 a Joint Select Committee of the Lords and Commons reported on the schemes submitted. The recommended scheme was essentially the same as Fowler had proposed the previous year. Three bills were quickly drawn up, and received Royal Assent on 29th July 1864. Two of these were for Metropolitan extensions, from Paddington to South Kensington and from Moorgate Street to Tower Hill (Minories). The third scheme was for a nominally separate company, the Metropolitan District Railway, to run from Tower Hill via Cannon Street, Charing Cross and Victoria, to connect with the Metropolitan at South Kensington. The District was to have its own parallel tracks from the last-mentioned point to Cromwell Road, continuing to Earl's Court, and with connections thence to the West London Extension Railway and West London Railway at West Brompton and Kensington (Addison Road) (now Olympia). There was also a direct connection from Earl's Court to High Street, Kensington, to make a further connection with the Metropolitan and complete the third side of the Cromwell Road triangle. The reason for having a separate company, which was initially completely controlled by the Metropolitan and was intended to merge with the Met in due course, was to enable it to raise more capital for construction than the Metropolitan alone would have been able to raise.

Construction of the Paddington to South Kensington section began almost immediately, but the task was more difficult and costly than the earlier line under the New Road, as the extension cut across the street pattern, and involved heavy compensation payments for damage or disturbance to property. At one crossing, at 23/24 Leinster Gardens, a dummy façade of two four-storey houses was built to avoid having an ugly gap in the terrace. There was a 421-yard tunnel through Campden Hill, but the majority of the line was in open cutting. Elimination of the broad-gauge tracks allowed the distance between the walls of the covered way to be reduced from 28ft 6in to 25ft, and a new construction method reduced the risk of subsidence or cracking in neighbouring buildings. Instead of excavating a 33ft 6in trench, a 6ft trench was dug on

Bayswater station at about the time of its opening, 1868. LT Museum

each side of the line, and the side walls built in brick to a height of about 10ft. Sufficient soil was removed to build a brick arch from one wall to the other, and the remaining soil, down to the future track bed, was then removed.

Stations were built at Paddington (Praed Street), Bayswater, Notting Hill Gate, Kensington (later High Street, Kensington), Gloucester Road and South Kensington. High retaining walls behind the outside platforms supported impressive arched roofs of wrought iron and glass, partially closed at the ends by semi-circular unglazed screens. The surface buildings were of generally similar design to those on the original section, and were single-storey, except for Gloucester Road, where there was a central second storey.

The eastern extensions of the Metropolitan have been described earlier, but, with its arrival at Aldgate in 1876, the Metropolitan finally lost enthusiasm for building cut-and-cover lines through expensive City property.

Back at South Kensington, the Metropolitan District Railway had, since early 1865, been making a painful beginning in constructing the authorised lines, and by 24th December 1868 when it opened between South Kensington and Westminster Bridge, had spent roundly £3 million, using up the whole of the share and debenture capital so far taken up. Three hundred men worked day and night to open the line in time for the Christmas traffic of 1868. By now, investors saw that the returns on capital were far lower than in the first days of the Metropolitan, and the collapse of the bank, Overend, Gurney & Co. in May 1866 led in turn to the collapse of the contractors Peto and Betts, one of the District's leading backers. The section from Paddington (Praed Street Junction) to Gloucester Road opened on 1st October 1868 and on to South Kensington and Westminster Bridge on 24th December. The intermediate stations between South Kensington and Westminster Bridge were Sloane Square, Victoria and St James's Park.

Further west, the connecting lines between South Kensington (west of station) and Earl's Court, continuing to West Brompton, and to Kensington (Addison Road), and direct between Earl's Court and High Street, Kensington were finished by summer 1869, but at first their only use was for a Gloucester Road–West Brompton shuttle from 12th April 1869. The District opened a separate station at South Kensington on 10th July 1871, completed by 19th July.

The District did not wish to complete the Westminster–Blackfriars section until it was receiving some income from South Kensington–Westminster, but the Metropolitan Board of Works pressed it to complete this section so that it could open its new embankment, with road and main sewer. The railway temporarily solved its financial crisis by obtaining parliamentary authority to issue Extension Preference stock, and under (Sir) Benjamin Baker, pressed on with construction so that the line to Blackfriars opened on 30th May 1870, with intermediate stations at Charing Cross and Temple, continuing via Queen Victoria Street to a station at the corner of Cannon Street known as 'Mansion House'. This opened on 3rd July 1871, laid out as a three-road (two island-platforms) terminus with facilities to fuel and water locomotives, and with sidings for them to stand outside the main tracks at the western end of the station.

Originally, all the District services had been worked by the Metropolitan locomotives and carriages, but the 1866 agreement gave the Metropolitan 55 per cent of gross receipts for local and through traffic. The number of District trains was fixed in the agreement, and the District had to pay for extra trains, so that ultimately it received only 38 per cent of receipts as net average payment. In mid-1869 the District sought independent advice, and the fateful choice was James Staats Forbes (1823–1904), general manager of the London, Chatham and Dover Railway (chairman and managing director from 1873). The advice favoured independence, and on 3rd January 1870 the District gave the necessary 18 months' notice of its decision to withdraw from the 1866 agreement. In the summer of 1870 the Metropolitan representatives resigned from the District board, and Forbes was appointed District managing director, becoming chairman and managing director of the company at the end of November 1872. In preparation for independence, the District ordered 4-4-0 tank engines from Beyer, Peacock of very similar design to the Metropolitan locos. The first twenty-four of this order were delivered in 1871, and subsequently six each in 1876, 1880, 1883, 1884 and 1886, making 54 in all. All the carriages were four-wheeled compartment type. The first class contained four compartments, and the second and third classes five. Trains were originally made up of two first, two second and four third class, but an extra second class carriage was added later.

The inception of independent operation was celebrated by a banquet on 1st July 1871, and public traffic to Mansion House began on 3rd July 1871. The two District platforms at High Street, Kensington were brought into use, and a so-called 'Inner Circle' service was inaugurated on that day between Mansion House and Moorgate Street via Kensington. The District and the Metropolitan each contributed an equal number of trains. Two further services followed in the next year – an 'Outer Circle' operated by the London & North Western Railway (which had contributed £100,000 towards Mansion House station) on 1st February 1872, from Mansion House to Broad Street. This 30-minute service followed the District line to Earl's Court, then via the District connection to Addison Road, then via the West London Railway to Willesden Junction and over the North London Railway (via Hampstead Heath) to Broad Street. The third 'Circle' was the 'Middle', another 30-minute service, operated by the Great Western between Mansion House and Moorgate Street. This followed the Outer

Circle as far as the junction from the West London line to the Hammersmith & City, then continued over the spur to Latimer Road, and round the H&C and Circle to Moorgate Street. The Inner Circle was extended to Bishopsgate and Aldgate when the Metropolitan inaugurated through running over these sections.

The Midland Railway, anxious to stimulate traffic on its new cross-suburban link between Cricklewood and Acton Wells Junction, began to run a through passenger service between Moorgate and Richmond on 3rd August 1875, with eleven trains each way on weekdays and six on Sundays. However, this was poorly patronised, and ran for the last time on 31st January 1876.

Shortly after the District's declaration of independence from the Metropolitan in January 1870, it sought to secure an early benefit of going its own way by constructing a new double-track connection across the Cromwell Road triangle. As the District owned the land within the triangle, it proceeded on the assumption that the connection, known as 'Cromwell Curve' did not need statutory authority. The line gave a second route between Gloucester Road and High Street, Kensington wholly on District tracks, and was completed on 5th July 1870, only to be temporarily cut by platelayers under instruction from the Metropolitan. Use of the curve by passenger carrying District trains started in July 1871 but ceased after two months. After arbitration of 27th July 1871, all the lines between South Kensington and High Street, Kensington were administered as the 'Western Joint Lines', with a fixed division of surplus revenue between the District and Metropolitan. Cromwell Curve henceforth had sporadic use, but the dispute flared up again in 1892, as we shall see.

The Metropolitan suffered a series of financial scandals in the late 1860s and early 1870s, and shareholder pressure resulted in Sir Edward Watkin (1819–1901) being appointed chairman on 7th August 1872. A man of long experience in railway administration, he had been general manager of the Manchester, Sheffield and Lincoln Railway from 1854, director from 1863 and chairman from 1864. From 1866 he had also been chairman of the South Eastern Railway, locked in seemingly endless battles with the London, Chatham and Dover (of which Forbes was Chairman), to the detriment of both railways' shareholders and passengers.

With these two autocrats, Forbes at the helm of the District and Watkin controlling the Metropolitan, much money and effort was wasted in fruitless legal battles between the two companies, which did nothing for the harmonious working of the Inner Circle.

The District was so heavily weighed down by having had to issue debentures to raise money for construction to Mansion House that it was unable to consider a further costly extension. Street traffic congestion east of Cannon Street was growing rapidly worse, and in 1873 the Metropolitan Board of Works proposed a combined street-widening and railway-construction scheme. A Mr G. G. Newman put forward a scheme, not merely to complete the Circle, but to link it with the East London, Great Eastern and North London Railways. The proposal was taken up by his company, the Inner Circle Completion Company, which gained parliamentary powers in 1874. It had promises of financial support for the road-widening elements of the scheme from two local authorities, but its attempt to raise capital, in October 1877, was a failure.

The Metropolitan had previously refused to collaborate with the District to complete the Circle, but changed its attitude when a supplementary scheme was advanced to build a branch from the Circle to Whitechapel, connecting with the financially-embarrassed East London Railway (opened from New Cross to Wapping in 1869, and on to Whitechapel and Liverpool Street [Great Eastern] in 1876). In May 1878 Watkin became chairman of the East London. Both the District and the

Outer Circle train at Mansion House on an 'outer rail' working. LT Museum

Metropolitan saw advantages in running through services to the two New Cross stations, and perhaps beyond. The Metropolitan and District Railways (City Lines and Extensions) Act was passed on 11th August 1879 for Circle completion, spurs to Whitechapel, and a running connection to the East London, including joint Metropolitan and District lines between Aldgate and Mansion House, and also to Whitechapel.

Negotiations brought modest increases in the contributions from the local authorities. The more affluent Metropolitan raised its share of the capital for the scheme, and promoted its own Act to build the Aldgate–Trinity Square section, which obtained Royal Assent on 3rd June 1881. There was a formal start of work on 5th September 1881, and the new line petered out at a wooden 'Tower of London' station, built in 60 hours. Some trains were extended thence from Aldgate on 25th September 1882. After some skirmishing between the Metropolitan and the District was settled, construction between Tower Hill and Mansion House began in autumn 1882, with the Metropolitan temporarily financing the work but offering to allow the District to become a financial partner at a later date.

An official opening ceremony for the completed Circle was held on 17th September 1884, and, after some experimental running, a public service round the whole Circle began on 6th October 1884, jointly run by the Metropolitan and District. There were also Metropolitan trains from Hammersmith (H&C) to New Cross (SER) via the northern half of the Circle, and Districts from Hammersmith (District) to New Cross (LBSCR) via the southern half.

Developments to 1906

With the opening to public traffic on 6th October, new stations were opened at Cannon Street, Eastcheap (renamed Monument on 1st November 1884) and Mark Lane. The Metropolitan reluctantly closed its Tower station after traffic on 12th October 1884. When the District later paid its share of the construction costs of the joint line, it refused to contribute anything to the cost of Tower station or dwellings built to rehouse the 'displaced working classes'.

The lines jointly owned by the Metropolitan and District were from Mansion House, round the Circle to just south of Aldgate station, and from Minories Junction (south of Aldgate) to St Mary's and round the curve to the junction with the East London (Whitechapel Junction). The District had a short piece of freehold track between the junction just east of St Mary's and its own Whitechapel terminus. Of the complete Circle of 13 miles, 7 miles 69 chains were Metropolitan property, 4 miles 4 chains District and 1 mile 7 chains joint.

The 1879 Act authorising the completion of the Circle Line had included a clause which was widely construed as imposing an obligation on the Metropolitan and District companies to operate services around the 'Inner Circle' route. As this was the immediate objective of both companies no great difficulty was foreseen and planning proceeded accordingly; it was only later when this obligation began to be felt onerous.

The initial timetable provided for eight Inner Circle trains per hour each way (instead of six for the old horse-shoe service), but, together with the other trains using the same tracks, this intensity proved to be beyond the capacity of the signalling system, and chaos reigned, as we shall see.

Although the District and Metropolitan had agreed to provide a joint service round the Circle (with a round-trip running time of 81–84 minutes), the District struck a pre-emptive blow by introducing 23 extra trains per day between Hammersmith and Mansion House with effect from 1st September 1884. When the public Circle service began, the signalling could not handle the scheduled 20 trains per hour between South Kensington and Mansion House, and on some days the whole service came to a standstill for several hours. The District also made matters worse by routeing its anti-clockwise trains over the Cromwell Curve, so that these trains had a flat crossing with the Metropolitan's clockwise trains at both High Street Kensington and South Kensington.

Henry Tennant, the general manager of the North Eastern Railway, was called in to arbitrate. At his suggestion, the attempt to run eight Circle trains per hour continued, with an 80-minute round timing, but with fewer pure-District trains on the South Kensington–Mansion House section, discontinuation of the use of Cromwell Curve on a regular basis, and the introduction of two Metropolitan trains on the Inner Rail (as well as the Metropolitan providing all the trains on the Outer Rail). This was introduced on 10th November 1884, and worked reasonably well. However, the District wished to increase its services from its branches over the trunk section, and after arbitration a 10-minute Circle service, with a 70-minute round-trip time, was introduced on 7th

The original Baker Street station building on the south side of Marylebone Road. Buses provided an alternative to the smoky sub-surface railway, but in Victorian times were more expensive. LT Museum

April 1885. There were seven Metropolitan trains on the Outer Rail, and two Metropolitan and five District on the Inner. The new timetable structure proved more realistic, and lasted for the remaining period of steam operation.

Although the concept of a continuous circular operation was superficially attractive, there were several practical disadvantages, the greatest arising from the use of steam traction. Before 1884, the locomotives could be serviced, inspected and watered at the termini of the horse-shoe service. When the trains ran on past the old termini, servicing and inspection had to be done on the Circle itself. The greatest problem was in discharging hot water from the locomotive tanks. This was heated when the locomotives had to 'condense' to reduce the emission of smoke and steam in tunnels. The exhaust steam was piped into their side tanks. This captured the steam and reduced the blast of air over the burning coal in the firebox, but the tank water was heated to boiling point, making it useless for condensing, and it is impossible to inject boiling water into a boiler. Therefore points were established on the Circle where a locomotive could be taken off a train for servicing and change of water, being replaced almost immediately by a new locomotive, freshly serviced and with tanks of cold water. These points were, for the Metropolitan, South Kensington for the clockwise service and Aldgate for the anti-clockwise service. The District locomotives were exchanged at High Street, Kensington. The procedure required the use of 'water-cranes' to fill the tanks quickly with cold water, and drains to remove the hot water. This had caused problems soon after Aldgate opened in 1876, as the locomotives discharged 218,000 gallons of water at 200 degrees Fahrenheit every 24 hours. Steam came through the road grilles, and brought obnoxious smells up through the untrapped water closets in surrounding properties. The Metropolitan had to pay for a special sewer to take the hot water directly to the River Thames.

The chaos on opening day, together with the ventilation problems and the childish inter-company rivalry, would in themselves have been good reasons for passengers to consider alternative means of transport, but two further factors combined to depress traffic levels. The advantages of the new through services from the two New Cross stations via the East London Railway had been grossly overestimated. There was no incentive for most of the London-bound passengers from the main lines to change at New Cross. The South Eastern Railway provided direct services to Cannon Street and Charing Cross, and London, Brighton and South Coast passengers could travel direct to Victoria or London Bridge, which was within walking distance of the City of London. The other factor derived from the peculiar geography of the eastern end of the Circle, which consisted of two parallel lines less than a mile apart, so that it was often quicker and cheaper to cut across the Circle by walking or taking a horse bus.

The lack of traffic on the completion lines brought a great deal of financial pain to the operators, as each company had to pay 4 per cent dividend on its share of the £1,250,000 capital cost. The pain was greater for the District, which had been running on an unsound financial basis since its inception.

King's Cross station in the 1870s, before the Circle had been completed but after the lifting of the broad gauge. The platform surface is made up of wooden planks and the lighting is by gas. Capital Transport collection

In these circumstances each company sought to gain every extra penny of income and to eliminate every penny of unjustified expenditure. Unfortunately, inter-company relations, under the autocratic direction of chairmen Forbes and Watkin, became so strained that recourse was had to lawyers to resolve differences which could have been settled directly by exercising a little goodwill. There were disputes about the District's share of interest on the capital of the Joint Lines, about fares and bookings, and about a District attempt, upon the expiry of 21 years from the 1871 agreement, to run 50 per cent of its share of the Circle trains over the Cromwell Curve. This dispute was not legally resolved until 1903.

The rivalry was manifest to the travelling public at the interfaces between the two railways. There were separate ticket offices at the joint stations, and from May 1886 the tickets for Circle journeys were available only by the route which involved the longer journey over the lines owned by the company issuing the ticket. There were also strident poster campaigns to persuade passengers to travel by one railway or the other.

The Metropolitan continued to order new rolling stock in small batches, and in 1889 three 9-car trains of 4-wheeled carriages, known as the Jubilee stock, were delivered, mainly for the needs of the extension from Pinner to Rickmansworth, but these trains were also used on the Inner Circle, releasing other stock for the Extension line.

Goods traffic over the Widened Lines burgeoned, but the Circle Line tracks only carried occasional Great Western trains from Bishops Road as far as Farringdon, where they crossed to the Widened Lines to access local goods depots or proceed south of the river. The Metropolitan did have its own healthy goods business north of Finchley Road, and to improve distribution to central London destinations (hitherto undertaken by road from Willesden Green) the Metropolitan opened its own diminutive goods depot at Vine Street (near Farringdon Street station) on 1st November 1909.

Charing Cross would have been fairly typical of a Circle station on the District Railway in steam days. In the centre is a typical signal box. LT Museum

Electrification

Operating frequent steam-hauled passenger and goods trains through a continuous tunnel without any satisfactory means of removing the products of combustion was bound to cause trouble. Such a tunnel existed on the Circle between Edgware Road station and just west of King's Cross; this had been planned when it was thought that a 'smokeless' locomotive, or normal locomotives with condensing gear, would emit little steam or smoke. The problem was not serious during the first few months of operation, as the service was comparatively infrequent, and the condensing water was changed each time the train arrived at Farringdon Street. However, with the increased service, and longer runs between changes of water, the atmosphere became ever more foul. As early as October 1865 the Board of Trade had asked Fowler to see how he could improve the ventilation, and eventually an extra shaft was built at Chalton Street (between King's Cross and Gower Street) in 1871. Some minor improvements were made elsewhere by removing glass above platforms and providing extra openings. These took the form of shafts crowned with iron grilles in the centre of the Euston Road and Marylebone Road, totalling eleven in number between Edgware Road and King's Cross. The unexpected blasts of smoke and steam spouting from these grilles not only frightened any passing horses, but could lift the skirts of any ladies standing on the grille. Some mechanical ventilation was put in, but most such installations had a short life.

The local authorities opposed still more vent shafts, and the Metropolitan experimented with systems of exhaust troughing both in the tunnel crowns and between the running rails, but neither system was practical nor economic. Eventually, in 1897, the House of Lords asked the Board of Trade to appoint a Committee of Inquiry. Various statistics were produced for the Committee, including the critical factors that 19 trains ran each way in each hour of the peak periods. The Metropolitan management brought out some extraordinary stories of the beneficial effects of the smoky atmosphere on their own staff affected with bronchial and asthmatic troubles. On the rest of the Circle, tunnel pollution was not quite so serious, as the line was built either in the open, or with large open gaps between tunnels wherever possible. The Committee recommended electrification, but that extra ventilation openings be permitted on a temporary basis. However, by the time that serious thought was given to this expedient, it was overtaken by the first practical steps to electrify the Circle.

When electrification beckoned, the impecunious Metropolitan District was the first of the Circle operators to obtain parliamentary powers to electrify. These were obtained in 1897, concurrently with powers to build a deep-level tube railway under the District from Earl's Court to Mansion House; both schemes had been urged on the District board by a powerful group of shareholders, though the deep tube proposal did not proceed in this form.

The Metropolitan secured powers for electrification in 1898. Much time was spent examining the few existing electric railways, and in considering offers to install experimental electric lines, which foundered when their advocates could not agree financial terms with the Met. The railway eventually participated in two separate experiments. One, a wholly Metropolitan affair, was on a long siding at Wembley Park, and experiments continued from autumn 1897 to summer 1900. This experiment utilised two separate conductor rails, outside the running rails, carrying current at 500–550V dc.

In May 1898, the Metropolitan and District agreed to conduct a joint experiment, between High Street, Kensington and Earl's Court. This was on a more substantial scale, and utilised six newly-built bogie cars, comprising four trailer cars and two motors. Current was generated by hired plant in a temporary power station west of Earl's Court station, and was supplied at 600V d.c. to two conductor rails positioned outside the running rails. The motor cars had four axles motored, but when the motor car was at the rear of a train, it was effectively a trailer, as all the tractive force came from the motor car at the head. This solved the problem of controlling the traction current for the rear motor car, but at the expense of providing and hauling a temporarily useless set of electric equipment. The motor cars had a saloon arrangement for the passenger accommodation, but the four trailers had conventional compartments. There were seats for 312 passengers, and a 6-car train weighed 185 tons. Experiments, outside traffic hours, began on the night of 7th-8th November 1899, and the general public was admitted from 21st May 1900, initially at a special fare of 1/- (5p) for one week, and then at normal fares until withdrawal after traffic on 6th November 1900.

Despite the archaic absence of traction from the rear car, the performance of the experimental train was deemed successful, and already, in May 1900, the two companies set up a joint committee to consider the results of the experiments. In late summer 1900 the committee invited nine firms to submit proposals and estimates to electrify the whole Circle.

At this stage events took a bizarre turn as the system rated highest by the two electrical referees was the one devised by Ganz and Co of Budapest. This used 3,000 volt three-phase alternating current and two overhead wires for each track. The referees saw an experimental installation in Budapest, and recommended it to the two boards on 7th February 1901. The main advantage of this strange and untried system was said to be its lower cost – there would have been only five unmanned substations, and new motor coaches could have hauled the existing steam passenger coaches. How the overhead wires carrying this high voltage could have been installed in the tunnels is not clear, and the complications in the overhead at subterranean junctions do not bear contemplation. Progress was halted by the Board of Trade demanding to see a test installation on the Circle itself.

The situation was revolutionised by the arrival of the American financier, Charles Tyson Yerkes, whose secret ambition was to electrify or construct as many London underground lines as possible and weld them into a monopoly. By February 1901, the financial world knew, in general terms, that an outsider was planning to acquire and electrify the District, and by June of that year Yerkes and his associates had gained control. They had experience of medium-voltage direct-current traction in the USA, and by April 1901 their dislike of the Ganz system became known. To resolve the matter they offered to electrify the Metropolitan or lease the whole railway and pay a guaranteed dividend on the shares. These offers were rejected by the Met and a Budapest visit by Yerkes did not change his opinion. The whole Circle line had to be electrified on the same system, which meant in practice that the whole of the Metropolitan and District electrified sections would have to conform.

The only solution was the arbitration provided by a clause in the District's 1901 Act. The companies agreed to proceed in this way in September 1901, and it was arranged by the Board of Trade as a tribunal under the presidency of the Hon. Alfred Lyttelton, KC, MP. Evidence was heard from both factions. The verdict was given in favour of the direct current system on 11th December 1901, with track voltage at 550–600V.

Both companies could now make a practical beginning with installing the new system, and each pursued its own course. In February 1902 the Metropolitan ordered equipment for a new turbine power station at Neasden and for 14 substations. The building contract for the power station was signed on 11th September 1902. The power station adjoined the Neasden locomotive and carriage works, where coal could be delivered by rail.

The Yerkes group was accustomed to planning on a large scale, and, at Lots Road, Chelsea, put in hand the construction of what was later claimed to be the largest traction power station in Europe to supply the District and the three Yerkes tubes. The main output of current, at 11kV, passed along cables to Earl's Court, and then to 24 substations, some of which were not commissioned until later. Initially, substations of both railways were equipped with rotary converters, rotating electrical machines converting the low-voltage a.c. current from on-site transformers to low-voltage d.c. output. Lots Road came into partial use on 1st February 1905, whilst at Neasden one turbo-generator was in use from mid-November 1904.

Both lines installed flat-bottom current rails to carry the traction current at 550–600V d.c. The positive rail was 1ft 2in outside the inner face of one running rail, and was normally between the two tracks in the tunnel sections. The negative current rail was between the running rails. Over most of the Metropolitan part of the Circle the track was relaid with hardwood sleepers to reduce the fire risk.

The other call for major infrastructure alterations on the Metropolitan was to install power distribution cables, and lengthen platforms at Gower Street, Edgware Road and Aldersgate. Some track improvements were made to improve operation, such as installing extra crossovers and providing direct entry to sidings, but only piecemeal improvements were made to the Metropolitan signalling. More comprehensive improvements were made a few years later.

Both companies wished to take advantage of electric traction as soon as possible, but the slow commissioning of the power stations slowed the pace of conversion. The Metropolitan began to run some passenger-carrying electric trains to Uxbridge from 1st January 1905, until all local trains to Harrow and Uxbridge were electric from 20th March 1905. On that day a trial run was made with an electric train between Aldgate and South Kensington.

The District insisted that electric operation round the whole Inner Circle should not begin before electric operation of their main line between Ealing Broadway and Whitechapel. The 1st July 1905 was selected for the great day, with electric operation of the Inner Circle's clockwise service. However, the plans were frustrated by a series of minor disasters. Torrential rain caused a flood at Hammersmith, and a train was derailed at Mill Hill Park. Worse was to come, for as soon as the Metropolitan's electric trains ventured on to the District, they promptly overturned the District conductor rails. This arose from the decision to fit the Metropolitan collector shoes to beams at the extreme ends of the bogies, so that on sharp curves the shoes were able to drop behind the District conductor rails. On the District stock, the shoes were mounted on shoebeams midway between the axleboxes, and the Metropolitan stock was hastily converted to the same layout. The Metropolitan had successfully operated an electric shuttle service between Aldgate and South Kensington on the planned first day, and this continued, at first between 10.00 and 17.00, but all day from 24th July. The full Inner Circle, meanwhile was still worked by steam, but there was a partial electric service round the whole Inner Circle from 13th September and a full service both ways from 24th September. The clockwise service was worked entirely by the Metropolitan with seven trains, and the anti-clockwise with five District and two Metropolitan trains.

On the District Railway's section, the London and North Western Outer Circle trains were hauled by pairs of District electric locomotives between Earl's Court and Mansion House, from 4th December 1905.

To make room for further increases in District Line services, the Middle Circle was withdrawn between Mansion House and Earl's Court after traffic on 30th June 1900, and between Earl's Court and Addison Road after traffic on 31st January 1905.

On the Hammersmith & City, a part-electric service between Aldgate and Hammersmith began on 5th November 1906, together with an electric shuttle between Kensington (Addison Road) and Latimer Road (now the last remnant of the Middle Circle), where connections could be made. Full electric services began on 3rd December 1906. They worked out of a new 20-train depot north of Hammersmith station, built by the Great Western but operated solely by the Metropolitan. Current was supplied by a Great Western power station at Park Royal, with substations converting it to 600V d.c. at Royal Oak and Shepherd's Bush. On 3rd December 1906 the shuttle service from Kensington (Addison Road) was re-extended to Aldgate with a service of four trains per hour and with one of these continuing to Whitechapel. From 31st October 1910 this shuttle was cut back to Edgware Road on weekdays, but with five 3-car trains per hour.

A steam train to Hammersmith passes a new electric train just outside Edgware Road station. Part of the Metropolitan's old repair facilities may be seen on the right, still in use, at least for stabling. Capital Transport collection

The main-line lessees of the East London Railway would not agree to pay for its electrification, so the through steam service between Hammersmith and New Cross (South Eastern) ran for the last time on 2nd December 1906. The following day saw the eastern end of the replacing electric service diverted to Whitechapel (District). The District service to the East London was withdrawn from 1st August 1905 and replaced by local East London steam services provided by the Brighton and (from 1906) the South Eastern & Chatham companies.

On the northern part of the Inner Circle, the GWR/Metropolitan steam trains between Aldgate and Richmond were withdrawn after traffic on 31st December 1906, 'replaced' by a Great Western rail motor between (Notting Hill and) Ladbroke Grove and Richmond which last ran on 31st December 1910. The Underground Group offered the Metropolitan compensation not to press for an electrified connection from the Hammersmith & City to the London & South Western viaduct towards Richmond, as the line west of Hammersmith was already overcrowded with District, South Western and Midland trains. This was accepted, and the connection was severed in November 1914 and completely removed on 7th May 1916 (by which time, perversely, there was ample capacity available to Richmond). In 1911 the Hammersmith to Aldgate service was eased slightly from the twelve trains per hour of 1907 to an average of ten.

The Great Western passenger trains which had run through from various GWR suburban stations to Aldgate began to be hauled by Metropolitan electric locomotives, instead of GWR steam, between Paddington and Aldgate from 1st January 1907, and this conversion was completed on 2nd September 1907. This left the only regular steam-hauled service over any part of the Inner Circle proper in the form of a Great Western freight service between Paddington (and points west) and Smithfield goods depot.

Reminiscent of the confusion that arose after the completion of the Inner Circle in 1884, the new electric service needed several adjustments before it settled down. Both the District and the Metropolitan were disappointed by the low level of traffic on the Inner Circle, but the District took the lead in reducing train lengths from six cars to four, backing its action by threats of financial sanctions against the Metropolitan if it ran longer trains of its own, and if it obliged the District to run longer trains. The change

Met electric trailer car shortly after delivery and prior to fitting with centre doors.
Capital Transport collection

A train of Hammersmith & City Railway joint stock at Hammersmith depot shortly after delivery. In later years the destination blinds were replaced by enamel plates and centre doors were fitted just after the First World War. LT Museum

was introduced in stages, with 5-car trains from 18th March 1907, and 4-car from 4th November 1907, with the Metropolitan supplying cars for the whole service. The 50 minutes running time that were allowed for the 10-minute service on the complete circuit from 2nd April 1907 proved inadequate, and this was soon altered to 55 minutes. The one-company allocation created a grave shortage of rolling stock throughout the electrified Metropolitan, and desperate expedients were adopted to maintain the services. The Inner Circle itself had a mixture of trains; some with a 150 hp-type motor car at each end, and others with a 200 hp-type motor car at one end and a first class driving trailer at the other. The first class passengers complained that they had no advance warning whether the first-class car would be at the front or rear of the train. From February 1909, the problem was solved by making an intermediate trailer in each set first class, and the driving trailer third class (by exchanging the internal upholstery).

A similar problem, with a similar solution, arose when driving trailers and 3-car off-peak trains were introduced on the Hammersmith & City in 1908/9, but in this case the conversion was on a lesser scale, as only the first class part of a composite car had its furnishings moved from the end to the middle of the train.

A South Kensington to Aldgate via Baker Street shuttle augmented the northern side of the Inner Circle with a 5-minute service from 2nd April 1907. The District returned to joint operation of the Inner Circle, supplying one-third of the cars, from 1st October 1908. This allowed a 6-minute service to be provided.

The Metropolitan and District constantly pressed the lessees of the East London Railway to proceed with electrification. In April 1911 the lessees agreed to share the cost of equipping the track, that the Metropolitan should provide the trains from its existing fleet, and that the District supply the power from an existing source. The Great Eastern agreed to find the capital, provided that the other lessees paid the interest in proportion to their responsibilities under the lease. Power came from Lots Road, being converted to traction voltage at an existing District substation at Whitechapel and a new one at Deptford Road (later Surrey Docks). Automatic electric signalling with a.c.

track circuits was installed, and operated from 30th March 1913, with the electric passenger train services starting on the following day. There were four 4-car Metropolitan trains per hour between South Kensington and Canal Junction, thence providing a half-service to New Cross (Brighton) and New Cross (South Eastern). The through trains were supplemented by local services of eight trains per hour between Shoreditch and the two New Cross stations. After 30th March 1913, Metropolitan trains no longer ran to Whitechapel (MDR) and from 9th February 1914, the through services started from Hammersmith (H&C) instead of Addison Road.

At Baker Street, the St John's Wood Railway of 1868 originally had a double line connection with the Metropolitan, but the congestion caused by the through trains between Swiss Cottage and Moorgate Street incurred the displeasure of the latter company, and the service was cut back to Baker Street from 8th March 1869. The double line connection (still needed for empty stock movements) was converted to single. This situation continued for 38 years, but from 28th January 1907 four trains per day ran through from the Extension Line to the City over what was now the northern part of the Inner Circle. The single-line connection again proved unsatisfactory and these trains were withdrawn in May of that year. Baker Street junction signalbox was resited and replaced in July 1909 by a power frame, which was itself displaced by a new cabin and 36-lever frame in 1913, on the east side of the north end of the Extension Line platforms. This allowed a more reliable service to be provided, and from 1st July 1909 there were twelve trains from the Extension Line to Aldgate in the morning peak, with a similar return working in the evening peak. Ambitious plans to rebuild Baker Street included a double-track junction, which was duly built. From 4th November 1912 a fortnight's trial working across the junction began, with the introduction at the end of this period of a new timetable with a greatly improved through service.

Aldgate station exterior, probably in the early 1920s. LT Museum

Westbourne Park station, Hammersmith & City Railway. LT Museum

Just as the Middle Circle had succumbed, so the Outer Circle trains were withdrawn between Mansion House and Earl's Court from 1st January 1909, as the District needed the line capacity on this section for its own services. At the other end of the Outer Circle, services were truncated from Broad Street to Willesden Junction in 1912, and through passengers were now obliged to change trains. The remaining part of the Outer Circle, the section from Earl's Court to Willesden Junction, was electrified in 1914 and LNWR (later London, Midland & Scottish Railway) trains continued to provide services on this section until 1940 when passenger trains were withdrawn from the West London Railway owing to wartime conditions – they were not to be resumed.

The heavy Underground traffic which built up during the First World War obliged the joint operators of the Inner Circle (it is now convenient to call it the Circle Line as the other 'Circles' were defunct) to lengthen the trains. The District's Circle Line trains were lengthened from four cars to five from December 1917, but similar changes to the Metropolitan trains had to wait a little longer.

Station reconstruction at Edgware Road was accompanied by a sweeping reorganisation at track level, which was influenced by a series of abortive schemes to build a deep-level relief tube between points west of Edgware Road and south of Willesden Green. These schemes failed for a variety of reasons, but Edgware Road gained a 4-track 2-island layout. Negotiations between the District and the Metropolitan resulted in the projection to Edgware Road of the District's Putney Bridge to High Street Kensington service, from 1st November 1926. These trains normally terminated in the two centre roads at Edgware Road. The Circle Line, henceforth to be operated wholly by the Met on weekdays, now had a 7½-minute service with a 52½ minute round running time. On Sundays there was a 10-minute Circle service, with a 50-minute round running time, and on this day of the week the District supplied two trains in each direction to balance the car-mileage between the companies. The supply of either one or two trains per direction by the District continued until 13th May 1990. The extended District Putney Bridge service was at 7½-minute intervals on weekdays and 15 minute on Sundays. The Hammersmith & City service was at 6-minute intervals on weekdays, and the shuttle from Addison Road to Edgware Road was at 20–24 minute intervals.

Another change affecting the Circle was introduced on 15th March 1926. It was devised as a method of enhancing the capacity of the northern side of the Circle, particularly in the eastbound or outer rail direction, by electrifying part of the City Widened Lines. A 700ft connection was made by cut-and-cover, branching north from the outer rail Circle Line at Chalton Street, and connecting end-on into the disused 1200ft tunnel of 1868 that lay across the front of St Pancras station. This, in turn, gave access to the Widened Lines just before the Midland connection came in. In the eastbound direction the whole route from Chalton Street to Moorgate was electrified on the standard 4-rail system. At Moorgate, two new Metropolitan 8-car platforms were built on a site created by evicting the LMS steam trains into the bay previously used by South Eastern & Chatham trains (withdrawn with effect from 3rd April 1916). In the westbound direction it was not possible to form a mirror-image of the eastbound without introducing a flat double-line junction at Chalton Street, so the electrification was taken only as far as Farringdon, where access could be gained to the inner rail Circle. Alternatively, trains starting from Moorgate could gain access there to the inner rail. This gave some flexibility of operation in the evening rush hour; in the morning peak the new arrangement gave extra capacity of eight trains an hour eastbound. The Chalton Street junction was controlled from King's Cross 'C' box.

Upon electrification the District had an entirely new signalling system, derived from that installed on the Boston Elevated Railway in 1900, and allowing the operation of up to 30 trains per hour. The great advance over normal block signalling was that, on plain tracks without junctions, the trains signalled themselves by means of track circuits, i.e. low-voltage electric currents flowing continuously through the two running rails. When a train was present, the current took the easier route through the train's wheels and axles. This change in voltage was detected by a special signalling relay connected to each track circuit. This caused the aspect of the signal behind the train to change from clear to danger, but it automatically reverted to clear when the train had passed. Signalboxes were needed only at junctions or principal reversing points. As an adjunct to the system, devices called 'train stops' were installed at each home signal. When the signal was at danger, an electro-pneumatic mechanism raised an arm at the side of the track; in its raised position this made contact with an arm suspended from the train bogie. This rapidly released compressed air from the train brake pipe feeding the Westinghouse brake system, so that the train came to a sudden stop if it ran past a red signal.

To improve train running, inner home signals were provided at some Circle stations in 1912, enabling a train to draw into a station more closely to the train ahead.

As soon as all the steam passenger services had been withdrawn from the Inner Circle, the minor step was taken of converting the existing distant signals to repeaters of home signals; some new homes were installed where they did not already exist. However, this change was not enough to cater for the improved acceleration and braking characteristics of electric trains, and an experimental automatic system was introduced in April 1907 between Notting Hill Gate and Praed Street junction. This used electric treadles and depression bars to operate Sykes' banner type signals. This type of signalling was later extended to South Kensington. However, because it could not detect a wagon that had become uncoupled from a loose-coupled Great Western freight train, it was disallowed by the Board of Trade east of Praed Street, and d.c. track circuits were installed between this junction and Aldgate, operational from 26th September 1905. There were variations in practice on either side of Farringdon Street station. On the west side, conventional short range colour light signals with d.c. track circuits were used. On the few open sections, the lenses were screened by hoods. East of Farringdon Street, the Metropolitan once more displayed its individuality by having lower quadrant signals activated by an electric pump driving oil through pipes leading to a double-acting piston, which moved the signal arm. Soon after installation, there was a wrong-side failure because of sediment in the oil, and the obvious remedy was adopted of having the electric motor drive the signal motion directly. Electrically-operated train stops were installed to operate in unison with all stop signals. The system of automatic signalling with treadles and depression bars between Praed Street and South Kensington was replaced by standard track circuiting from 22nd June 1919.

Signal cabins at Praed Street junction (July 1909) and Aldgate (September 1909) had power frames. Intermediate boxes kept their mechanical frames. All new installations from 1913 had a.c. track circuits. A new box at Baker Street opened in 1924, with 39 working levers and 7 spare.

An important year for signalling improvements on the Metropolitan section was 1926. A new signal box with a 44-lever mechanical frame was built at Moorgate and that year also witnessed a rebuilt box at Aldgate, extra levers at King's Cross 'C', and a 35-lever electric power locking frame at Edgware Road, which allowed the closure of Praed Street Junction box as part of the station reconstruction referred to earlier. At about the same date, the Widened Lines were resignalled throughout with two-aspect colour lights with fog repeaters.

In 1932 the signalling of the original line between Baker Street and Farringdon was updated with modern colour-lights. On the Hammersmith & City section, the Metropolitan arranged for automatic signalling to be installed between Hammersmith and Westbourne Park, operational from 17th December 1922, but the Westbourne Park to Paddington section was not converted until 1929. Platform lengthening also called for rebuilt signal boxes at Aldersgate and Farringdon, both in 1932.

The Circle Line did not have the benefit of rolling stock built for its own special needs, but had to rely on the large fleets of new electric cars acquired by the District and Metropolitan.

The District electric stock was rigidly standardised, and the fleet consisted of sixty 7-car trains of the open saloon type, classified as 'B' type. There were three motor cars

District Railway electric B Stock dating from 1905. Trains of these cars made up the District's contribution to Circle Line operation. LT Museum

First class car of 1913 Circle stock as delivered. LT Museum

and four trailers in a standard train, but various train lengths were soon operated with different combinations of cars, and trains on the Circle Line were always somewhat shorter. The design was very similar to that of the cars on the Boston Elevated Railway, but with bogies and couplers to a Chicago design. Many were built in Belgium and France. There were double sliding doors in the centre of each car side, and single sliding doors at each end.

The Metropolitan took a more orthodox approach to its rolling stock ordering. It ordered the new saloons in three batches, adjusting the designs and numbers of cars in the light of experience. This resulted in a variegated fleet of 82 motor cars and 152 trailers, which required constant attention by the engineers to keep the electrically incompatible batches separate. The first batches were ordered with open end platforms and without any doors in the body sides – completely unsuitable for the intensive short-distance traffic of the Circle. These major defects were later expensively rectified, when the platforms were enclosed and middle doors inserted, but major incompatibility between batches persisted.

Because of joint ownership with the Great Western, the Hammersmith & City service was operated by a small fleet of jointly owned electric stock (half the stock belonging to each company); there were twenty motor cars and forty trailers, twenty of which were later converted to driving trailers. Each car carried the titles 'Great Western & Metropolitan Railways' on the white-painted cantrail on one side of the car and 'Metropolitan & Great Western Railways' on the other. The waist rails were also white, and the rest of the exterior bodywork varnished teak, similar to the style used for the early electric saloon stock owned wholly by the Metropolitan. The white paint discoloured quickly in the presence of steam locomotives, and the white sections were soon replaced by a standard teak finish. This stock remained on the Hammersmith & City until eventually displaced by more modern cars in the late 1930s. When service extensions were made subsequently, the joint fleet was augmented by Metropolitan stock.

For a short time some of the District's contribution to the Inner Circle was provided by four trailer cars with an electric locomotive at each end, but from 1st June 1910 these locomotives were given a less demanding role in hauling the occasional through Ealing–Southend/Shoeburyness trains between Ealing Broadway and Barking.

The electrification of the East London Railway and the development of through services from the Extension Line across Baker Street called for more rolling stock, and extra saloon cars were ordered by the Metropolitan in 1912. After delivery, these cars were known as 1913 stock. Forty-three cars were supplied by the Metropolitan, Carriage, Wagon and Finance Co Ltd. There were 23 third class motor cars, ten third class trailers and ten first class driving trailers. The car bodies were generally similar in layout and furnishings to the original electric stock of 1905, but central side doors were provided on all cars from the outset, and elliptical roofs displaced the clerestory roofs of the earlier stock. Sufficient electrical equipment was ordered for the new motor cars, but in practice some was swapped with that on the 1906 electric locomotives. Most of the new cars were pressed into service on the Inner Circle, with some of the older stock transferring to the East London.

Great increases in the demand for passenger transport in London followed the First World War, and the transport operators had to examine how their fleets could be augmented. The Metropolitan responded with an order placed with the Metropolitan Carriage Wagon & Finance Company for 20 motor cars with three pairs of double doors per side (one pair next to the luggage compartment being slightly narrower), and 33 third class and 6 first class trailers, all with three pairs of double doors per side. The bogies and motors were recovered from the original 20 electric locomotives, and all motor cars had British Westinghouse equipment. Motor cars seated 37 passengers, first class trailers 45 and third class trailers 50. Delivery began in December 1920. This partly steel-bodied stock was used mainly on the Circle. All the Metropolitan trains on the Circle had been increased to 5-car length by 24th January 1920. By 1930, the Metropolitan's rolling stock position had been further eased by new stock for the extension line, so that it was able to transfer four 6-car trains of 1905 vintage to the Hammersmith & City, where they remained for the rest of their working lives.

Inner Circle train leaving Farringdon Street on the 'inner rail' in May 1927. The Widened lines are plunging down towards the left and it may be seen the 'up' road is electrified for the use of Metropolitan trains. H.G.W. Household

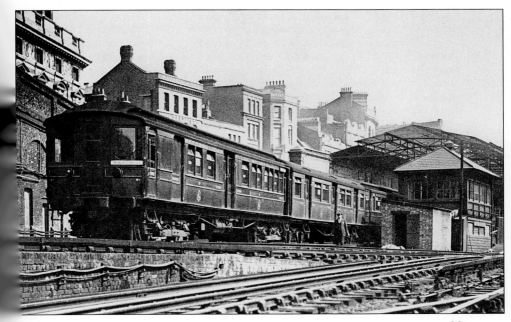

Infrastructure Improvements

In the years after electrification the Metropolitan Railway became increasingly concerned about the poor traffic receipts on the Hammersmith & City which it attributed to the joint working with the Great Western, which brought a 'main line' approach to the administration. A new agreement of 31st December 1912 gave the Metropolitan control of the Hammersmith & City train services and maintenance of the way and works, from 1st January 1913. The Met would spend between £20,000 and £100,000 on infrastructure improvements, and have a large degree of freedom to fix fares. This was followed by a further agreement of March 1923, under which the Great Western ownership of half of the 60 cars was sold to the Metropolitan Railway, and Hammersmith depot was leased to them. The Joint Committee still existed, and the Metropolitan Railway charged it a mileage payment to work the line.

Numerous station improvements were effected between the original opening dates and the end of the period of private ownership, particularly in the quarter century immediately following electrification. During this period, the majority of the arched overall roofs were demolished, and replaced by separate platform canopies. There was also a tendency to rebuild ticket halls at basement level and redevelop the street buildings with office and retail letting in mind; this was usually done in conjunction with the building of subways beneath some of the busier roads. Platform lengthening was another cause for changing station arrangements, and at a few stations changes to track layout required some rebuilding work.

On the District and its joint line portions various stations had surface buildings rebuilt in more modern style, including Cannon Street (1910), Mark Lane (1911), Temple (1896 and then more comprehensively in 1915), Embankment and High Street Kensington (1907). At the last-mentioned station, a large and imposing glass-roofed shopping arcade was built with an octagonal hall for the ticket office and direct access to the local departmental stores. At Embankment (by then Charing Cross) there were subsequent improvements and an enlarged ticket hall and an intermediate basement-level concourse were in use from 4th December 1928.

Monument (1919) and Mansion House (1912), South Kensington (1907) had station buildings rebuilt at basement level. At the latter a small shopping arcade now linked Thurloe Street and Pelham Street. A pedestrian subway between South Kensington station and a point in Exhibition Road just south of the present Imperial College Road opened on 4th May 1885, but from 10th November, was available for special events only. It was opened for toll-free access on 21st December 1908. At Mansion House there were modifications to the platform layout in 1910–11 whereby the north side (ex-LNWR) bay road formerly used by Outer Circle trains was swapped over with the westbound platform so that trains reversing there did not conflict with through movements. The Mansion House station entrance was rebuilt in granite and Portland stone in 1928.

St James's Park received a second entrance in Palmer Street in 1910, and there were other major alterations caused by the building of the General Offices (later

Paddington (Praed Street) station as rebuilt by the Metropolitan in 1914. LT Museum

Electric Railway House) in 1897; the station was rafted over when a new block of railway offices were built above the platforms in 1924. The main station entrance was comprehensively rebuilt soon afterwards, nestling under a multi-storey building intended to give the Underground yet more office space. The block, '55 Broadway', was so large that, on its opening on 1st December 1929, four floors were rented to tenants. As part of this scheme, the station stairways were widened and the platforms lengthened.

At Westminster, a pedestrian subway to the Houses of Parliament was opened in 1870, but not opened to the public until 1934, concurrently with a public stairwell on the south side of Bridge Street. In December 1906 a second entrance was opened on the Victoria Embankment; the reconstruction of this small entrance in 1924 was Charles Holden's first work for the Underground, and was followed by a complete reconstruction of the main ticket office.

At Blackfriars the covered way to the Chatham station, then known as 'St Paul's' was opened on 13th November 1886.

On the Metropolitan-owned section Paddington (Praed Street) was an early example of the Metropolitan's policy of rebuilding its inner London stations, and the official date of completing the reconstruction was 25th May 1914. The use of biscuit-coloured faience in classical style created an imposing new street elevation. It was designed by the Metropolitan's staff architect, Charles W. Clark.

Edgware Road was rebuilt in 1911, and modifications were made at Great Portland Street (Portland Road until 1917), which received a new exit staircase in 1877 and a new ticket office in 1884.

Baker Street, mentioned above in connection with the 1912 double track connection between the Extension Line and the Circle, was such an extensive installation that it was subject to constant tinkering. The separate small station buildings, north and south of the Marylebone Road at Baker Street, were demolished. The northern building was replaced by a triangular structure, with stairs to a subsurface booking office (completed 1913), leading to the eastbound Circle platform, and linked to the westbound by a bridge, providing an early example of the use of reinforced concrete and dating from 1911. An ambitious plan to rebuild Baker Street in a manner befitting a main line railway was approved by the Metropolitan board of directors in January 1910, The 200ft single storey building was erected behind an elevated cab road and was planned to be the first stage of a 400ft frontage incorporating a huge property development, at one point intended to be a hotel and restaurant. A foundation stone was laid in 1912; it was to be 1929 before the whole project was completed. This massive scheme finally emerged as a block of residential flats (known as 'Chiltern Court') and was resumed in August 1927 with some tenants having moved in by the end of September 1929, although another year had to elapse before the interior was finished. The railway improvements incorporated in the scheme mainly affected the Extension Line station, but there were two extra passageways between platforms 1 and 2 and the outer rail Circle platform, and reconstruction of the Circle Line entrance at Marylebone Road/Upper Baker Street, completed on 28th June 1930.

Previously, the expected additional traffic created by the Wembley Exhibition of 1924 had prompted the construction of an additional Circle Line entrance and ticket hall on the south side of Marylebone Road, opened in April 1923.

King's Cross originally sported a very large overall roof of glass and wrought iron, of 80ft span and 264ft long. This covered the three platform faces, with the station buildings at the west end, linked by a gallery and bridge across all tracks to booking offices in Gray's Inn and Pentonville Roads. With the construction of the City Widened Lines in 1864–67, the two Great Northern platforms had to be squeezed in, with the eastbound platform a little to the east of the others. After that there were few alterations for about 40 years. King's Cross gained an interchange subway between the Metropolitan station and the forecourt of the Great Northern main line terminus, on 20th June 1892, which was extended to the Piccadilly Line station in 1906. However, a major upheaval was caused by the London County Council's scheme to replace horse-drawn tramcars by electric cars, which required a direct route from Caledonian Road to Gray's Inn Road. The desired link was given by a new ferro-concrete skew bridge, but its construction involved demolishing many of the existing station buildings. New buildings, including a booking office and shops, opened on the west side of the new bridge in 1911. The decrepit overall roof was demolished and replaced by umbrella roofing on the island platform and cantilever type roofs on the side platforms. A separate booking office and entrance was built in Pentonville Road for the City Widened Lines passengers in 1912.

At Moorgate the overall roof had deteriorated so badly that a dangerous structure notice was served in 1893. It was removed in 1894, and replaced by umbrella canopies on the individual platforms. A new street level building was available for Metropolitan passengers from 17th June 1896.

At Liverpool Street (Bishopsgate until 1909) the 80ft-span glazed overall roof was demolished in 1911–12, and replaced by a steel and concrete raft which, at street level, supported a new shopping arcade running from Old Broad Street to Liverpool Street, and about 300ft long and 18ft wide. This was eventually tenanted by 27 shops selling a wide variety of goods. At the west end was a new booking office, refreshment rooms and circulating area. Access to the arcade could be obtained from either end. The official opening date was 11th March 1912.

Royal Oak station had been opened on 30th October 1871, when the extra tracks were opened between Westbourne Park and Paddington and little happened for many years, apart from the construction of an island platform in 1904 to replace the two side platforms. Westbourne Park, opened for the Hammersmith line with wooden buildings on 1st February 1866, was completely rebuilt to serve the Great Western line as well, opening on 1st November 1871, with a very long street façade on the overbridge. After the 1913 agreement, a street canopy was erected by the Met.

Ladbroke Grove (Notting Hill and Ladbroke Grove from 1880 until 1919) had virtually fallen to pieces from neglect by 1900, and was completely rebuilt in 1900–02. Here, the 1913 agreement resulted in a street canopy and a new booking office on the eastbound side. The isolated Latimer Road had a new platform shelter and reconstructed buildings in 1914.

A new, wooden station on the west side of Wood Lane, just south of the bridge carrying the Hammersmith & City over Wood Lane itself, was opened on 1st May 1908, to serve the Franco-British exhibition, held in the White City grounds which adjoined the station. The station was well patronised as long as annual exhibitions were held at White City, but closed after traffic on 31st October 1914, and was subsequently opened on special occasions only.

The old Shepherd's Bush station, between the Uxbridge and Goldhawk Roads, was replaced by two stations from 1st April 1914; a new Shepherd's Bush on the north side of the Uxbridge Road, and a new station, Goldhawk Road, on the south side of that road. The approach roads to the old station, and some of the arches beneath the viaduct, were converted for use as a retail market, which opened on 29th June 1914. The Shepherd's Bush ticket hall was within one arch of the viaduct and the Goldhawk Road ticket hall within two arches. Street entrances were on each side of the bridge abutments.

Royal Oak station with a GWR parcels cart outside.

A few years after Portland Road station became Great Portland Street in 1917, the appendage '& Regents Park' was added. This view shows the diamond style of name sign used by the Metropolitan. LT Museum

In similar circumstances to those at Ladbroke Grove, the wooden structure at Hammersmith was found to be disintegrating, and a handsome new brick terminus was designed by the Great Western architect, P. E. Culverhouse, and erected in 1907–09. The terminal tracks were shortened to provide space for an enlarged concourse. The existing platforms were replaced by two new ones (a side platform and an island) with three terminal tracks. The new red brick buildings incorporated shops and staff rooms. On the Beadon Road frontage was a canopy for the full length of the façade, a large clock on a pediment, and a small cab road. In 1912 a large free-standing circular booking office was built in the concourse, replacing the old one in the frontage, which was replaced by shops. A narrow passageway between shops led to another entrance in Hammersmith Broadway opposite the District station. Facilities were further enhanced by an electric train indicator.

On the poorly-patronised Addison Road branch, Uxbridge Road station (opened 1st November 1869 and well sited to serve Shepherd's Bush) lingered on until 19th October 1940, when its career was brought to a sudden end by German bombing. Addison Road, Kensington, opened on its present site on 2nd June 1862, was subject to numerous track and platform changes during its long career. It originally had platforms and station buildings on the east side of the line only, but the west side was completed on 1st October 1869, and an additional booking office opened there in 1872. The arrival of Olympia exhibition hall in 1886 made the west side more important (the station buildings were badly damaged by World War II bombs, and their replacements were concentrated on the west side).

In the early 1920s the Metropolitan embarked on a grand 'double-naming' programme, doubtless to entice the unwary to use its stations when they could often have found a more convenient Underground Group station. The jointly-owned Hammersmith & City Railway offered up the first example of this when the 'Notting Hill & Ladbroke Grove' of 1880 became 'Ladbroke Grove (North Kensington)' on 1st June 1919. When the process got under way in earnest 'Farringdon Street' became 'Farringdon & High Holborn' on 26th January 1922, 'Aldersgate' of 1910 became 'Aldersgate & Barbican' in 1923, 'Bayswater' became 'Bayswater (Queen's Road) and Westbourne Grove' in 1923, 'Great Portland Street' of 1917 had '& Regent's Park' added in 1923, and King's Cross (Metropolitan) had '& St Pancras' added in 1925. The District generally stood aloof from the 'double-barrel' movement.

After the completion of the Metropolitan's new office block in Allsop Place (Baker Street) in 1914 and the reconstruction of Paddington (Praed Street) station in the same year, further progress had been stopped by the outbreak of World War I. The station programme was resumed as soon as possible after the end of the war, with the new station buildings being designed by C. W. Clark, to a generally similar pattern with light-biscuit coloured faience to represent stonework, and a severely rectangular pattern of windows, shop spaces, and entrances in the 2-storey station buildings. Farringdon was completed in November 1923, Aldgate in 1926, Edgware Road in 1927/8, Notting Hill Gate in 1928, Great Portland Street in 1930 and Euston Square in 1931. The Aldgate reconstruction was comprehensive. At street level an illuminated canopy, a tea shop, buffet and two other shops were provided. Further inside the station was a 20ft by 55ft booking hall, with parcels and left luggage offices and a ladies' room. A 20ft-wide staircase led down to a large circulating area, whence two staircases descended to each platform.

Euston Square was a difficult station at which to lengthen the platforms as this photo, taken in August 1930, shows. The view is looking east, towards the existing platforms.
Hulton Getty

London Transport

Throughout the 1920s there was pressure for better passenger transport facilities throughout the London area, and the received wisdom was that railway development could not be economically justified in the areas of greatest need unless all of London's public passenger transport were amalgamated into one huge board. Notwithstanding Metropolitan Railway resistance, a Bill eventually received the Royal Assent on 13th April 1933, and the new Board took control of both the Metropolitan and the District Railways, amongst much else, on 1st July 1933. At last the whole of the Circle Line was under a single ownership and management. The Board also took over the Metropolitan's interests in the Hammersmith & City Railway.

In the meantime the District Line had in 1932 been extended from Barking to Upminster via a pair of additional electrified tracks alongside the LMSR's existing Tilbury and Southend line; all this had increased traffic phenomenally. Unfortunately there were major bottlenecks which preventing further augmentation of services; these included the existing pattern of train services and the awkward siting and inadequate size of Aldgate East station. In the peaks, nine trains per hour from the Hammersmith & City service had to negotiate the two flat junctions on the northern and eastern apexes of the Minories triangle (North Curve Junction and Aldgate East Junction respectively) before joining the main District Line, and then negotiate two more (St Mary's Junction and Whitechapel Junction) to join the East London Line south of Whitechapel for New Cross and New Cross Gate.

This pattern did not cater for the demands of the majority of passengers. In the evening peak most passengers already on an eastbound Hammersmith & City train alighted at Aldgate East and waited on the crowded platform there for a District train to Barking or beyond. The ends of the Aldgate East platforms were prolonged by narrow 'cat-walks' in the first part of the tunnel, but physical constraints prevented full width platform lengthening. There was the further complication that neither track from North Curve Junction or Minories Junction to Aldgate East Junction could satisfactorily accommodate an eight-car train. This all needed to be sorted out, as will be related shortly.

In the meantime, extra rolling stock was needed to augment train services between Aldgate East and Barking, which was achieved by diverting two-thirds of the Hammersmith & City service to Barking instead of the East London Line. Although some revolutionary ideas for the design of new surface stock were being developed, the immediate need for new trains was urgent, and cars of a District design of 1931 were ordered, 14 motor cars and 14 trailers. This was classified as Class 'M', and 26 similar trailers of Class 'N' were also ordered.

On delivery, the Class 'M' cars were marshalled in four 6-car trains, with four spare cars. They began to enter passenger service in spring 1936. Two of the trains were fitted experimentally with air-operated sliding doors, and passenger-operated door buttons, allowing passengers to open individual doors. This augmentation of the fleet enabled there to be an experimental diversion of some Hammersmith & City trains to

A train of new 'M' stock, delivered in 1936 for the Hammersmith & City Line.
LT Museum

Circle Line stock as refurbished in 1934.
LT Museum

East Ham on 30th March 1936, and Barking on 4th May 1936, coinciding with the withdrawal of first class accommodation from the East London and Hammersmith & City lines on the same date.

This diversion to the Barking line was immediately popular with the travelling public. The East London local service was augmented by shuttles between Shoreditch and the two New Cross's. From the Hammersmith & City Line, in the peaks, eight trains per hour ran to Barking and four to the East London. There were no through trains to the East London in off-peak periods. Improved interchange facilities were provided at Whitechapel, with a new staircase down from each District island platform to the 'northbound' East London platform (which was for much of the day used by trains in both directions).

Another important step taken by the young LPTB was to assemble a dedicated fleet of cars for the Circle. Ninety of the most presentable of the ex-Metropolitan fleet of saloon stock were selected, and sent to Acton Works in 1934 to be given extensive modernisation treatment. Eighteen 5-car trains were assembled, each in the formation M-T-T-T-M. All 59 cars of the 1921 Stock were included, plus four trailers of 1905 Stock, with the balance made up of 27 cars from the 1913 batch.

Most of the work was concentrated on the bodies. The luggage compartments were converted to seating areas, and end communicating doors installed, so that passengers could be detrained through the train in emergency. Light fittings were rearranged and given bell-type shades similar to those of the current tube stock. The 18 first class cars (former control trailers with the equipment removed) were furnished with loose cushion upholstery, and the third class with fixed upholstered seats trimmed in moquette. The cars were painted internally in the standard Underground 'cerulean blue' (in fact a dark green) and cream, and externally in red with cream upper panels. As with earlier attempts to run trains on the Circle with extensive areas of cream paint, the excessive maintenance costs of keeping the cream looking presentable dictated a change of policy, and the external livery was soon changed to a rather uninspiring overall red. Hand-operated sliding passenger doors were retained throughout.

When the first refurbished train was displayed to the Press, it carried boards on the car sides just behind the driver's cab saying 'Circle'. However, traditions die hard on the Underground, and the destination boards carried at the car ends announced that the trains were 'Inner Circle' until this stock was withdrawn. The first rehabilitated train entered service on the Circle on 8th March 1934.

In the accountant's textbook, railway rolling stock should last up to 40 years. The London Transport of 1933 had few examples of surface stock as old as this, but for many of the cars inherited from the District and Metropolitan railways, the time for retirement was fast approaching. The archaic layout and equipment of some groups of cars also made prompt replacement desirable.

At about the time that London Transport was considering fleet replacement, it was approached by the Metropolitan Vickers electrical company to try out a revolutionary way of controlling traction current on multiple-unit trains. This took the shape of a very heavy rotating electrical machine which supplied a constant current at a variable voltage, under the name of a 'Metadyne'. After tests on two cars, these machines were installed in a 6-car train of ex-Metropolitan saloon stock which ran experimentally on the Circle Line (mostly on the clockwise service) between summer 1935 and late 1936.

The experiments were deemed successful, and the Metadyne was fitted to a huge fleet of new surface stock, primarily intended for the Hammersmith & City (the 'O' stock) and Metropolitan Lines (the 'P' stock). The 'O' stock was easily recognised by having the guard's position in the driver's cabs at the extreme ends of the trains, while the 'P' stock had the guards position at the car ends remote from the driver's cab, as on contemporary tube stock. The most urgent requirement was to replace the former jointly-owned cars operating on the Hammersmith & City Line and it was decided to purchase 116 new cars, all with Metadyne control. These were intended to be entirely Motor cars formed into 58 semi-permanently coupled 2-car units with automatic couplers at the outer ends where the driving cabs were located and one set of metadyne equipment supplying both cars. Trains were to be made up of three such units where 6-car trains were required, though shorter trains could be formed off-peak. All these cars had characteristic flared sides, designed to avoid the need for external running boards. The 'O' stock was delivered from September 1937 to late summer 1938.

While the new trains were being built it became clear that they would be overpowered and among the other difficulties this would cause it was doubted that some of the substations could cope. The problem was addressed by purchasing 58 trailer cars which allowed the same number of the 2-car units to be made up to 3-cars, of which there would now be two per 6-car train. Motor cars rendered surplus by these new arrangements were redeployed on the Metropolitan Line where they were incorporated in its 'P' stock trains.

The Circle Line has always been difficult to operate. Unlike other lines which run from one terminus to another, there is no point at which enough layover time can be scheduled to provide a recovery margin for late running. Although some pauses, not normally exceeding 3½ minutes, are scheduled during the course of negotiating the complete Circle, these cause delay to through passengers and are insufficient to recover more than marginal lateness. The scheduled pauses, when added to the scheduled running time, must give an overall figure for the circuit into which the service interval must divide exactly. In addition, the rolling stock is worked intensively, and there are numerous flat junctions with other lines. After the formation of the Board, one of the new authority's first actions was to seek Parliamentary powers to escape from the statutory obligation to run a continuous service on the Circle, whose origins lay in ancient history.

The Board's Bill for 1933–34 sought to repeal the relevant clause of the 1879 Act. The Borough of Kensington discovered that the western section of the Circle would be replaced by a shuttle service between South Kensington and Edgware Road or Baker Street. Frank Pick, Vice-Chairman of the LPTB, wrote to Kensington Council on 27th April 1934, promising that, when South Kensington station was reconstructed, the Board would arrange for cross-platform interchange between the shuttle and the District Line, for both directions of travel. He also promised that the shuttle would never run less frequently than the current Circle service, i.e. every 10 minutes on Sundays and in the early morning and late night periods on weekdays and every 7½ minutes at all other times. The Board would contemplate running a 4½ minute shuttle service in the weekday peaks, subject to traffic justification. In the meantime, there would be no change to the Circle service until the new facilities were provided. Kensington was eventually persuaded to accept the position after receiving some key assurances. The Bill received Royal Assent on 31st July 1934.

One of the most troublesome junctions on the Circle had been just east of South Kensington station. Here Clockwise Circle trains had to cross the eastbound District Line. The timetable was constructed to allow this crossing to be made without delay, but if trains ran out of sequence or late then severe delays could be caused to the District service when a Clockwise Circle waited for a gap in the eastbound District service, so delaying westbound District trains following behind. In its Bill for the 1934–5 Session the Board sought to acquire powers 'to construct a flyover junction at Cromwell Road, South Kensington, so as to bring the Circle trains into direct platform connection with through trains at South Kensington station'. This would have been achieved by having a compromise flying/burrowing crossing scheme west of Gloucester Road. The eastbound District line would have been slewed to a maximum of 59 feet further north, and raised on a low embankment until it was about 6 feet above the westbound track. At its summit it would have crossed both Circle tracks by a bridge, these tracks having been lowered in a cutting by a maximum of 8 feet 5 inches below their original level. The two Circle tracks continued eastwards to South Kensington between the two District tracks, but no plans were officially deposited for this station, as no statutory powers were required here. Presumably cross platform interchange between the shuttle and District trains in both directions would have been achieved by making the two Circle tracks terminate in a single track between the two platforms used as an existing Metropolitan bay road, and diverting the through District tracks to serve the outside faces of the same platforms. The Bill received Royal Assent on 2nd August 1935, but, apart from renewal of the powers, no further action was taken.

The Circle Line had already been a late arrival on the Underground map, as its parents, the Metropolitan and District Railways, had monopolised the map for many years. This was not surprising, as main line maps covering more than one railway had always distinguished the individual lines by ownership. Services were so complex that it was neither necessary nor practicable to show the individual services on a map which might cover half the country. The same applied to the Underground map as long as the network gave hospitality to such services as the Middle and Outer Circles. When these disappeared, there was an opportunity to help strangers by showing the Inner Circle distinctively, but the first steps towards this objective were hesitant and faltering. An Underground Group map of 1919 showed the Circle by a shaded green line, but this had disappeared by the 1922 issue. The Metropolitan card maps produced for the Empire Exhibition at Wembley (1924–25) showed it as a mixed red-blue line, on the District section, but red on the Metropolitan (the standard colours used were red for the Metropolitan and blue for all other underground railways). It was not shown separately on the Metropolitan paper maps.

After London Transport took over, there were proposals to integrate the Metropolitan and District services. Presumably with the idea of catering for every possible permutation of linking, both the Metropolitan and District were, from the No. 2 map of 1937, shown on the Underground diagram in a single green colour which included the Hammersmith & City and East London lines and stretched out to Aylesbury. This continued until the poster maps of 1947 and the folder map of 1948 when the sections of line used by the Inner Circle were outlined with thin black lines; this was explained in the key as 'Inner Circle'. However, the 1949 poster and folder maps showed the Metropolitan reverting to purple, with the District staying green. The Circle was shown as a separate yellow line bounded by thin black lines, parallel to and inside the Metropolitan and District on common sections. The word 'Inner' was finally abandoned, 15 years after the prototype-rehabilitated train had plain 'Circle' on the car sides.

Soon after the Board was formed, ideas were put forward to take advantage of the new-found common ownership by integrating the surface services into very long through services, such as, possibly Richmond–Uxbridge via the Circle Line between South Kensington and Baker Street. However, all kinds of operational difficulties were apparent, the most serious being that, the longer the service the more difficult it would be to keep time. The Underground management hankered after an eastern shuttle (serving Aldgate), and there were ideas at one stage of special platform arrangements at Aldgate East to facilitate interchange for displaced Circle passengers, and at another stage for a rebuilt Monument to allow trains to terminate there from the east, which was a non-runner because of the high cost of approach flyunders. Thus, pursuit of the chimera of scrapping the Circle was put aside, but the thought still lingered.

Accidents on the Circle Line have been few, but at about 09.55 on 17th May 1938, an Inner Rail train comprising five cars ran into the back of an Ealing–Barking District train of six cars of 'C' stock just after leaving the then Charing Cross station towards Temple. The trains collided with considerable force, so that telescoping took place between the two rear cars of the Barking train, with the underframe of the rear car mounting that of the fifth car for a distance of about 15 feet. Six passengers were killed and 46 injured. Although structural damage to the colliding train was described as 'trifling', in practice the first car of the Circle train (built 1921) and the last car of the District train (built 1911) were scrapped as being beyond economical repair.

Signal modernisation work (converting d.c. track circuits to ac) had been taking place on the preceding Monday night/Tuesday morning, but a signal linesman had restored the connections incorrectly, so that, instead of there being three successive track circuits beyond Charing Cross which had to be free of trains before the starting signal would clear, only one circuit had to be clear before the starting signal was given, thus allowing successive trains to approach each other too closely.

The Inspecting Officer found that acts of omission by several groups of staff contributed to the accident. The original fault was with the signal installer, but the failure of the chief linesman to test the controls after installation was the primary cause. Signal faults were reported by motormen up to 18 minutes before the collision, but the station staffs at Charing Cross and Temple had not appreciated the seriousness of the situation, and had failed to warn drivers of following trains to proceed with extreme caution. The collision was discussed at length in the Board's annual report for 1937/38. It was described as the first such collision fatal to passengers since one at West Hampstead in 1907. Strangely, there had been a collision on the Northern Line between Waterloo and Charing Cross less than two months before, on 10th March 1938, also due to linesman's error. Twelve passengers had been injured.

The increase in use of 8-car trains along both the north and south sides of the Aldgate triangle proved an intolerable burden on an already very awkward junction. The fouling movements were bad enough but when trains were held – as they often were – their rear ends still sat across the preceding junction bringing everything to a halt. The solution settled upon involved shifting Aldgate East station further east and using the vacated station site to extend the berth tracks so that long trains could wait for their path without getting in the way of other movements.

Resiting Aldgate East station has been described as one of the largest and most intricate railway works ever carried out in London, at least at that time. The new station had entrances at each end, compared with an entrance at one end of the platform only at the old station. A new double-track south curve was built in tunnel between the west end of the new Aldgate East station and Minories Junction. The old south curve tunnel became redundant. The new north curve mainly followed the existing alignment, but with some minor deviations to the north between the old and new Aldgate East stations. The new Aldgate East station opened on 31st October 1938, and the new south curve four weeks later. Nine hundred men were employed during the weekend of the main changeover.

The new east entrance to Aldgate East was considered to be a suitable replacement for St Mary's station which closed to traffic on 30th April 1938. The track south of Aldgate station (where the work enabled the southbound platform to be lengthened and the layout improved) was girdered over to provide a large coach station and a turning place for the trolleybuses then being introduced to replace trams.

The new Board had inherited a very mixed bag of stations. Many were archaic, both in design and decoration, but physical and financial limitations precluded wholesale reconstruction. The improvement schemes of this period were therefore confined to the reconstruction of the ticket offices and their immediate surrounding.

Monument gained extra importance when it was elevated to the status of an interchange station by the opening of a widely-publicised connection to Bank station on the Morden-Edgware line on 18th September 1933. There was a long subway from beneath the west end of the eastbound District platform which led to two MH-type escalators, descending 60ft to tube platform level. This was shown on Underground maps as an 'escalator connection', and also connected, after a long subterranean walk, to the Central London and Waterloo & City lines.

The platform walls were tidied up by being lined with white enamelled-iron plates, marked in panels to carry advertisements and station name bull's-eyes. This work was completed in 1935, and a contract was placed to build pedestrian subways beneath the Cannon Street/King William Street/Gracechurch Street intersection, financed by the City of London, and opened on 2nd December 1935.

The old King's Cross Metropolitan station, which occupied the site of the present-day Thameslink platforms until 1941. LT Museum

Further west, there was not much building activity, except at Sloane Square, (a deeper than average station on the Circle Line), where a scheme had been announced as early as 1927 to rebuild the ticket hall and install an 'up' escalator from the westbound platform to street level. By 1930 a proposed new eastern entrance had been added, but this was not pursued. By September 1936 the Board had approved a scheme with an escalator from each platform, which included lengthening both platforms towards the west so that the escalators could rise from near the platform centres. Work started early in 1938, and now included 'easing' the down stairways by introducing intermediate landings. At street level, the new, spacious ticket hall would include a modern buffet. The rebuilt Sloane Square station, with its two new escalators, opened on 27th March 1940.

A scheme to rebuild and enlarge Gloucester Road station petered out. However, High Street Kensington was extensively rebuilt at street level, with a new ticket hall further south than its predecessor. Upon leaving the ticket hall, ingoing passengers passed along a new passenger bridge to stairways to the platforms. The work was completed on 2nd July 1939, and gave room to expand the shopping arcade.

In October 1934 reconstruction of Paddington (Praed Street) was well in hand. Reconstruction of the booking hall had begun and a new concrete-beam floor was being laid. There was also a new staircase from the ticket hall to the Great Western subway. The rebuilt booking hall and Praed Street entrance were completed in January 1935.

King's Cross was most inconvenient for Underground interchange, with the Circle station being remotely sited to the east, in the same complex as the Widened Lines station, and linked to the tubes and main-line termini by a long interchange subway. For the tubes, there were separate stations for the Morden-Edgware and Piccadilly lines. Under the umbrella of the 1935–1940 New Works Programme, a bold scheme was conceived to bring all the Underground stations together with the tube lines linked by escalators to a common booking hall. The Circle station was to be moved westwards and connected to the booking hall by a short subway. The Circle scheme involved use of the tunnel built in 1868 beneath the front of St Pancras station but never used until the 1925 Metropolitan scheme to electrify part of the Widened Lines. A platform and running line would be built in the tunnel for outer rail trains, and the original double running tunnel would be used for a single track bay road to project off-peak trains from Baker Street. An entirely new tunnel would be built for the inner rail running line and platform. All platforms were on the same level and connected by cross-passages. At the east end of the platforms was a concourse with a small booking office and a flight of stairs to the subway to the street and to the tube booking hall. The tube part of the scheme was completed on 18th June 1939, but the Circle part was not implemented before the outbreak of war.

At Aldgate, a comprehensive improvement scheme, under way in August 1935, embraced the main entrance to the ticket hall, the ticket office and the staff rooms. The ticket office had a new glazed front and the interior was modernised. The old parcels office/cloakroom was converted into three new rooms – a stationmaster's office, a porters' room and a switch room. Modern fittings were installed.

Paddington, Bishops Road, the historical station that had served the original Metropolitan Line of 1863, lost its separate identity on 10th September 1933 when the platforms were simply renamed 'Paddington', as part of a plan to rebuild and rationalise Paddington main line station (although LT internally continued to use the old name until the following year). After rebuilding was completed, Bishops Road had four platforms (two islands) 630ft long, instead of two at 315ft, and these platforms became numbers 13–16 of the new station, or Paddington (Suburban) as it was informally called. The arrangement offered at least some passengers from the terminating Great Western steam trains the luxury of cross platform interchange with the Hammersmith & City. An engine siding was provided at the east end of the station, for the electric locomotives to await their through trains to the City from the western suburbs and beyond. A new ticket office, with passimeter, was built at street level to serve the Bishops Bridge Road end of the islands (the old station building was demolished), and a connection to the main station was provided by a new steel footbridge, which carried another small ticket office, sited over platform 8.

Another move by London Transport was to ignore the appendages added to the station names by the Metropolitan Railway. King's Cross St Pancras survives for pragmatic reasons, and Aldersgate and Barbican clung on until the 1960s, but for all practical purposes the rest had gone by 1938.

Although some piecemeal signalling improvements were made during this period, the most significant improvement was the construction of an 83-lever signalbox south of Cromwell Road, on the east side of the eastern leg of the triangle. By operating one push-pull miniature lever, the signalman could set the signals and points for a train to pass through the whole area. The areas controlled were commissioned in four stages – Cromwell Curve and 'depot' (21.6.36); Earl's Court (east) (9.8.36); High Street Kensington (6.9.36); and Earl's Court (west) (20.9.36). This was the largest installation of route-setting signalling on the Underground at that time. Although only 33 of the levers were of the push-pull type, they controlled the vast majority of train movements.

A through Uxbridge–Barking service was started on 17th July 1939 as a means of sending 8-car rather than 6-car trains to Barking; this allowed the Hammersmith service to be concentrated to East London Line destinations. An early wartime timetable change was the withdrawal of nearly all the remaining Hammersmith & City services to New Cross or New Cross Gate, from 29th November 1939, apart from a very limited number of journeys, which were themselves withdrawn from 6th October 1941. From this latter date, the Hammersmith & City peak hour service was once again extended to Barking in place of the Uxbridge to Barking peak service which was cut back to Aldgate. As we shall see in a moment, aerial bombardment caused the northern side of the Circle to be blocked for many months, so this service had only about a month and a half when conditions had been normal. This lengthy but brief service had amply demonstrated the operational problems which arose from very long services crossing many others on the flat.

Wartime

After the outbreak of war on 3rd September 1939, its effects were evident after dusk by the total blackout of open stations, and of trains serving the open sections. From 23rd September there was some car lighting from three tiny dark blue lamps in each car, and some very dim lights on stations. Pressure resulted in the authorities agreeing to special safety reading lamps, which were manufactured and installed in the cars within 14 days of approval, but the result was not apparent in trains until January 1940.

The Circle Line was wholly in central London, and as this area attracted the most concentrated bombing when the Blitz started, the whole line was in a target area and suffered disproportionate damage. Apart from direct hits on the line itself, the tracks could be too dangerous to use because of partly-wrecked buildings adjoining the line. The reasons for line closures were many and varied. Straightforward hits with high-explosive bombs could cause immense damage, and fire-bombs raging firestorms, but perhaps the most frustrating were the unexploded and delayed-action bombs, where the site had to be evacuated until they had been exploded on site or made safe by the services' bomb disposal teams. Much bomb damage could be repaired and so allow the service to be resumed within a few hours, but the durations of closures had infinite gradations, up to a closure of several months if there had been a direct hit on a vital part of the railway infrastructure. One such incident occurred at Goldhawk Road on 19th February 1944 when a high-explosive bomb partly demolished the plate girder bridge. Services resumed on 21st February with single line working.

On 19th September 1940 a bomb penetrated the tunnel roof between Euston Square and Great Portland Street, damaging a train, killing two railwaymen and injuring some passengers. This activity resulted in suspension of all services across Baker Street until 10.50 on 26th September.

Next came a direct hit on the Clerkenwell Tunnels (between King's Cross and Farringdon) at 03.40 on 16th October. The Widened Lines tunnel (known also as the Granville Tunnel) collapsed, and the extent of the repairs needed caused train services to be suspended until 30th March 1941 inclusive. The bomb's weight was estimated at 1,000kg. In the same raid, King's Cross (Met) station was damaged and remained closed until 9th December.

On the night of 20th/21st October 1940 the West London Line was heavily bombed. The east side of Addison Road station was severely damaged, as was the section of line connecting the Hammersmith & City Line to the West London. This spelt the end of the Edgware Road–Addison Road shuttle, the last vestige of the Middle Circle (this did not normally run on Sundays, so its last day of operation was Saturday 19th October). It never ran again.

A horrific incident occurred at Sloane Square on the evening of 12th November 1940. A crowded train was departing when a high explosive bomb fell directly on the station, causing extensive damage. A large piece of concrete fell right through one car. There were 79 casualties, plus three people who just disappeared. The new escalators were completely wrecked, and train services were not resumed for a fortnight.

Sloane Square station, which had recently been modernised, during the clear-up operation after bombing on 12th November 1940. LT Museum

Bomb damage at Aldersgate station (today's Barbican) following the heavy bombing of the City on 29th/30th December 1940. LT Museum

Moorgate station after the heavy bombing of 29th and 30th December 1940. LT Museum

The 29th-30th December 1940 will always be remembered for the great fire raid on the City of London. Large parts of the City were burnt out, but bombs also fell as far west as Westminster, South Kensington and Shepherd's Bush. The whole of the Aldersgate-Moorgate area was set alight, and the fire engulfed Moorgate station. A 6-car train of 'O' and 'P' stock, stabled in one of the bay roads, was completely burnt out and had to be written off. The raid also put paid to the LNER and LMS services over the Widened Lines to Moorgate (then interrupted by the Granville Tunnel closure) which were not resumed until the end of the war. Farringdon, Mark Lane, Blackfriars, Whitechapel and Aldersgate stations were closed because of damage to the stations or adjoining property. As there were no raids the following night, the repair gangs were able to reopen many sections of line, but 24 hours later closures still affected Mansion House – Aldgate East and Aldersgate – Moorgate.

On 9th March 1941 there was widespread damage at King's Cross, where the Circle and Widened Lines platforms still stood side-by-side. A train, the station roof and the platforms were badly damaged. Two railwaymen were killed, and two railwaymen and one passenger injured. As the new Circle station 300 yards further west was virtually complete, permission was obtained from the Ministry of Transport to open the new station in an unfinished state, and the opening took place on 14th March 1941, before the formal Ministry inspection on 21st March. The opening had originally been planned for 6th April. A temporary signalbox was installed at the west end of the old platform, to replace the one at the east end destroyed in the air raid on 9th March. The central bay road in the new station had track but no conductor rail or signalling.

The final major attack on London with conventional bombers took place on the night of 10th-11th May 1941, and the northern part of the Circle was again in the front line. One bomb penetrated the tunnel west of King's Cross station and another landed nearby. The tunnel arch was badly fractured and displaced, causing settlement of the tunnel. A train was damaged, and the Circle Line blocked with debris. The service was suspended between King's Cross and Baker Street but on 21st July an automatic reversing crossover was introduced at the east end of Euston Square station, allowing trains to reverse from the west. Finally, through running to King's Cross was resumed on 4th October 1941.

There were other events on the night of 10th-11th May. A bomb between nos 2 and 3 roads at Aldgate closed the station for 11 days, although the Mark Lane – Aldgate section of track reopened on 14th May. At Baker Street a bomb landed between nos 3 and 4 roads, damaging two trains so that a 'P' stock driving motor car had to be written off. The damaged tracks were restored by 12th May. St Pancras main line terminus suffered some direct hits, and one bomb penetrated the basement and exploded 25ft down in the solid clay, behind the wall of the tunnel used by the LMS Widened Lines trains (freight only at this time). As the clearances in the tunnel were very tight, it was possible to restore services on 27th July, before repairs were complete, by interlacing the two tracks for 200 feet, with signalling arranged for single-line working. The interlacing was removed on 28th December, but the single-line signalling arrangements remained until 18th January 1942. On the District section, feeder cables in the tunnel between Victoria and St James's Park were damaged, and an unexploded bomb outside Victoria station compelled the line to be closed for seven days.

From July 1941 the scale of air attacks diminished, and 1942 was relatively quiet. 1943 and 1944 brought renewed attacks, followed by the V1 flying bombs from 13th June 1944 and the V2 rockets from 8th September. However, conventional bombing continued intermittently.

Refurbished Circle Line trains passing at bomb-damaged Moorgate in 1948. LT Museum

Post-War Developments

Although the Hammersmith & City Line was blessed with modern 'O'-type stock, the post-war Circle Line had been obliged to soldier on with the stock rehabilitated in 1934. This consisted mainly of cars originally introduced in 1913 and 1921, but there were also five veteran cars dating from 1906 (some substitutions had taken place since 1934).

The withdrawal of this collection of mobile museum pieces was made possible by the delivery of a fleet of 90 new aluminium-alloy 'R' stock cars for the District Line. This allowed the transfer of the 1920 'F' stock to the City–Uxbridge service of the Metropolitan, which in turn permitted the transfer of some 'P' stock from the Uxbridge service to the Circle. All these movements took some time to implement.

The first steel-and-wooden-bodied trains were withdrawn from the Circle on 17th February 1947, but the final withdrawal was not until 31st December 1950. The 'P' stock trains were in 5-car sets, normally consisting of four motor cars and one trailer (M-T-M+M-M). These trains did not achieve any increase in reliability over their predecessors, and the constant stopping and starting took its toll of the Metadyne machines. Some spare PCM (pneumatic camshaft mechanism) control equipments were available, and as an experiment this equipment was substituted for the Metadyne on one train. This was of mixed 'O' and 'P' stock, and entered service on the Circle in June 1955. The experiment was successful, and it was decided to convert all the 'O' and 'P' stock similarly. The Circle Line cars were dealt with first, and the first train of the 'production run' entered service there in September 1957. The Circle Line was completely converted by December 1958, its fleet comprising fourteen trains for the needs of the timetable and three spares. The converted motor cars were designated 'CP', and when the 'O' stock was subsequently converted, from May 1960 to January 1963, the motor cars became 'CO', with the trailers 'COP'. All conversions were done at Acton Works.

The 5-car trains on the Circle became unreasonably overcrowded, and it was possible to lengthen them to six cars by inserting a trailer car into the 2-car unit in each train. The extra trailers had been released by converting 'Q38' trailers from the District, where the fleet was strengthened by introducing three new trains of 'R' stock. Longer trains began running on the Circle from June 1959 to January 1960, and 6-cars has remained the standard.

Wartime had seen Britain's railways (including the Underground) come under 'temporary' government control after which formal nationalisation took effect from 1st January 1948. A British Transport Commission was established to which reported various functional executives devoted to particular aspects of the Commission's activities; a London Transport Executive was created to look after the activities of the former London Passenger Transport Board. None of this had any major impact on London Transport's day-to-day activities though it is probably fair to say that, certainly in the early years, it provided a stable funding regime within which many worn out wartime assets could be replaced. The Commission was a very unwieldy body and was broken up on 1st January 1963, with London Transport established as a Board reporting at first directly to the minister, and from 1st January 1970 (again restyled Executive) to the Greater London Council.

Organisationally there were some changes of ownership during this period which affected the Hammersmith & City service. From 1948 the Hammersmith & City Railway between Westbourne Park and Hammersmith transferred entirely to the London Transport Executive while at the other end of the service the track and stations between Bromley and Barking remained under main line ownership until 1st January 1969 (Barking station excluded), although the track itself was resignalled and managed by London Transport from 1960. Following transfer the stations very gradually began to take on a London Transport 'feel' as signs and equipment were updated.

On 12th November 1967 the Hammersmith & City trains were segregated from those of British Railways (Western Region) between Royal Oak and Paddington, and within the main line terminus. These trains now used platform 15 westbound and 16 eastbound, leaving platforms 13 and 14 to the Western Region suburban trains. The operators attained their objective of complete segregation, but passengers lost cross-platform interchange between LT and BR at Paddington; Royal Oak island platform was henceforth served solely by LT trains. The track and stations (but not Paddington ticket office) were formally transferred to London Transport from 1st January 1970, by which time the entrance to Paddington (suburban) from Bishops Bridge had closed (with effect from 4th June 1969). It was in part replaced by a makeshift footbridge from the Bishops Bridge cab road into the side of the suburban ticket office.

An 'O/P' stock train ('P' stock leading) at South Kensington prior to track rearrangement in 1958. The 'Inner Circle' name survives half a century after it became irrelevant.
LT Museum

The Circle Line benefited from a significant proportion of post-war expenditure. The bridge where the Circle Line, on its way from King's Cross to Farringdon, emerges from the southern Clerkenwell Tunnel and flies over the Widened Lines tracks has always been known as the Ray Street gridiron. The original structure, erected in 1866–67, was made of wrought iron, and it also acted as a strut between the retaining walls. The wrought iron deteriorated under the effect of locomotive smoke, and was replaced in 1892/93 by a new cast-iron structure to support the Circle tracks, but it did not strut the retaining walls. In 1945 and 1958 movements were noted in the retaining walls, and the initial remedy was to stabilise the walls by gradually building a mass concrete invert, 180ft long and 28ft 6in wide, beneath the Widened Lines tracks.

However, continued deterioration of the iron led to replacement of the grid-iron (comprising thirteen 25ft girders), by a continuous reinforced-concrete raft, 108ft long, and acting as a continuous strut. This work was carried out in 1960.

At South Kensington and Gloucester Road an outside undertaking provided the incentive for a major track reorganisation. It will be recalled that a 1934 plan for a flyunder west of Gloucester Road station was abandoned because of cost and uncertainties about the eastern side of the Circle. However, the problem did not go away, and in this case it was air transport that helped to start things moving.

In the 1950s, air transport operation was on a very small scale compared with today, and it was then thought essential to make the majority of passengers book in at a central London terminal and be despatched to London Airport by coach. British European Airways was about to be evicted from its existing terminal at Waterloo, but it enjoyed cordial relations with London Transport, and a scheme was evolved for a West London Air Terminal and office block. The site chosen was above the Cromwell triangle west of Gloucester Road. The reason given for selecting this site was that it was the only large vacant site in inner west London.

The terminal was built on a concrete slab supported on vertical steel stanchions, with the slab being at the same level as Cromwell Road. Its construction obliged the Underground to reduce severely the number of stabling sidings within or adjoining the triangle, and to remove the historical Cromwell Curve twin tracks. New sidings, under the west side of the Air Terminal, had to be threaded between the stanchions.

At the same time, a revised track layout was introduced between the triangle and South Kensington. The Outer Rail Circle and the 'fast' eastbound District exchanged tracks, and the Outer Rail and the eastbound District had a flat crossing west of Gloucester Road. The Outer Rail trains still split off from the westbound District trains just east of South Kensington, but they now had a track to themselves between that point and the flat crossing, so that any pausing to await a gap in the eastbound District service no longer delayed the westbound District service. The scheme also had the advantage of providing a single eastbound platform at both Gloucester Road and South Kensington, instead of passengers having to choose one of two platforms to take the first train going east. The main alterations were introduced on 28th July 1957.

The former clockwise Circle track was used by eastbound District trains non-stopping Gloucester Road and South Kensington, but this final fling of a time-honoured practice came to an end with the District timetable of 12th October 1964. This left the non-stop track vacant, so, just west of South Kensington, a plain running connection was made from the former anti-clockwise Circle and District 'slow' track to the former fast track. This came into use on 8th January 1967, and enabled all eastbound trains to serve the north side of the island platform at South Kensington. From 30th March 1969, the divergence point of the westbound District and Outer Rail Circle was moved to just

In this east-looking view the new route to Moorgate underneath the Barbican development can be seen under construction, with the existing route on the left.
LT Museum

west of South Kensington, so that all westbound trains served the south side of the island platform. At Gloucester Road, the island platform was widened over the roadbed of the former District fast track and extended 84ft east, so that from 1st March 1970 all eastbound trains used the north side of the island, and clockwise Circles continued to use the south side. The westbound District trains had their own platform on the south side, but a crossover at the west end of the island enabled them to use the island platform and regain their own tracks towards Earl's Court in emergency or at times when the service was infrequent.

A property development scheme arising from massive wartime destruction in the City was to affect the north side of the Circle. The Barbican redevelopment scheme, promulgated by the Corporation of the City of London, aimed to build a new zone of cultural and residential redevelopment. Between the then Aldersgate station and Moorgate station, the parallel Circle and City Widened Lines made a curving sweep to the north, followed by a sweep south to enter Moorgate station. This section was partly in open cutting and partly in tunnel. A plan, evolved jointly by London Transport and the consulting engineers to the City Corporation, was for a new, straight underground link between the two stations, to modern constructional standards. Apart from shortening the Circle and City Widened Lines, this greatly simplified the work of redeveloping the Barbican area, and the City Corporation agreed to meet the cost of building the railway diversions. Work began in September 1963, and had advanced far enough for the first track relinkings to take place in June 1965. The first Circle train used the realignment on 6th December that year.

Aldersgate & Barbican station was renamed simply 'Barbican' on 1st December 1968, as being more appropriate for the large residential and cultural centre which had been built to its immediate east. Its standard Metropolitan overall glazed arched roof had been badly damaged during the war, and was demolished early in 1955, to be replaced by utilitarian low-level platform awnings. Its passing was greatly regretted by Sir John Betjeman, the Poet Laureate, who wrote a poem to commemorate the passing of the old station (Monody on the Death of Aldersgate Street station). Sir John also commissioned a watercolour painting by David Tindle, which he presented to the London Transport Collection in 1974.

With the increasing age of the structures supporting the roadways over the Circle Line's covered ways, and the ever-increasing volume and weight of road traffic, replacing or strengthening the supporting girders or brickwork had become a virtually never-ending task. Back in 1939, the iron- and steel-work where the Metropolitan ran beneath Smithfield Market had deteriorated and was replaced by new steelwork, each piece enclosed in a brick waterproofed chamber. Now, early in 1968, a new Ministry of Transport code for bridges and structures called for a review of the roofs over cut-and-cover sections. Work on the first eight sections was due to be completed by the end of 1968. The strengthening was done by fitting pre-stressed concrete roofs or inserting additional steel beams. Phase I began in Tothill Street, Westminster (between St James's Park and Westminster stations) in June 1968. Up to four new beams were erected in one night beneath Parliament Square. By February 1969, work was in hand on the section where the Circle and District ran beneath Victoria Embankment. Here, 150 yards of tunnel roof between Horse Guards Avenue and Derby Gate had to be removed initially.

In east London, the running of the Hammersmith & City trains to Barking was improved by the implementation of two major projects in connection with the long-promised electrification of the London, Tilbury & Southend line. Barking station was completely rebuilt in 1961, and the approach tracks on each side were redesigned from scratch, with a breathtaking series of flyunders and flyovers that allowed cross-platform interchanges but avoided conflicting train movements.

The other major scheme was the complete resignalling of the 12½ track miles used by Underground trains between Bow Road station and just east of Upminster Bridge station, where the area controlled by the Upminster box was reached. The resignalling, to the standard London Transport two-aspect system, was planned in five stages, starting from Bow Road in October 1959.

The Aldersgate sidings, used at one time for transfer movements between the Circle and the City Widened Lines, were closed progressively. The shorter siding (rarely used since the lengthening of trains to 6-cars) and Circle Line crossover were removed in 1971, the 6-car siding and Widened Lines connection in April 1979, in connection with the electrification of the Widened Lines for the Midland trains.

In the mid-1950s the operation of the southern half of the Circle was speeded up by the installation of speed-control signalling between Sloane Square and Mansion House. By installing extra signals and automatic speed checking devices, it was possible to allow trains to approach more closely a train ahead standing in a station platform. The system was gradually removed in the 1970s because of its extra maintenance costs and a reduction in the frequency of the scheduled service.

Goods services had begun their slow decline before the Second World War with the LMS depot at Whitecross Street closing in 1936, spelling the end of goods trains east of Smithfield.

At the western end of the Hammersmith & City line, the provision of goods services reflected the line's joint origin as part of the Great Western Railway. There was a separate goods station at Hammersmith, and some alternative access routes were available. As already mentioned, the BR and LT tracks were interconnected at Paddington (suburban) station and Royal Oak until 1967, but for many years there had been a direct connection from the Great Western down main line just east of Westbourne Park station direct to the Hammersmith & City, all at surface level, and known as the Crystal Palace loop. For many years Hammersmith was served by a nightly freight train, which ran up to three times a week, and which reversed at Latimer Road to serve Kensington (Olympia) where there were large yards.

However, these freight services ceased using the West London from June 1952, and the Latimer Road spur was closed on 1st March 1954, together with the Latimer Road signalbox. The Crystal Palace loop was reduced to a siding from 15th January 1956. Hammersmith goods station closed on 1st February 1960, and the relevant adjustments to track, points and signals were made on 21st April 1963. The sidings at Westbourne Park, formerly connected to the Hammersmith & City (Crimea and Portobello sidings), were abolished from 20th November 1967, and the (H&C) signalbox there closed from 7th March 1971.

A working that had imported a little variety to the Circle disappeared with the closure of High Street Kensington goods yard from 15th November 1963. In happier days, a 3F 0-6-0 tank engine and coal wagons had left the ex-Midland main line at Brent Junction and proceeded via Dudding Hill, Acton Wells Junction, Turnham Green, Hammersmith and Earl's Court.

The final goods working from the Widened Lines to Blackfriars via Snow Hill was in the shape of a parcels train from Holloway to London Bridge and return, which ran on 23rd March 1969. These workings normally used a banking engine from Farringdon to Holborn Viaduct, for which London Transport extensively revised the signalling arrangements in 1958, allowing an increase in the maximum number of wagons in a train from 30 to 50.

The goods working most apparent to Circle Line passengers had been that from the Western Region to Smithfield goods depot, sited on the south side of the Widened Lines between Farringdon and Aldersgate. A 'condensing' tank hauled a maximum of twenty-five 4-wheeled meat wagons and a brake van from Paddington (H&C) as far as Farringdon, where it used a crossover just west of the station to move over to the Widened Lines. Just west of Aldersgate it reversed into sidings linking into the Smithfield depot. This comprised six sidings, of which four were connected by turntables worked by hydraulic capstans. A hydraulic lift took the goods up to the main market. The return train working to Paddington left the depot at its western end and followed a similar routeing to the inward movement. The Smithfield goods working (in later years conveying chilled and frozen meat almost exclusively) was powered by diesel locomotives from 1960, but was completely withdrawn after the final working on 28th July 1962.

Our attention must now turn to the passenger services over the City Widened Lines, which nearly followed the goods services into oblivion. As mentioned earlier, the passenger services were suspended during wartime. Restoration was piecemeal. The London & North Eastern Railway was the first off the mark, with services to Aldersgate from 1st October 1945, as Moorgate was still too badly damaged to handle the Widened Lines passenger traffic until 6th May 1946. The London, Midland & Scottish trains to Moorgate were reinstated on 7th October 1946.

Moorgate in about 1961 showing an inner rail Circle Line train departing, 'T' and 'A' stock trains in the bay roads and a diesel loco waiting in the layby siding outside the widened lines platforms. In this view the tracks curve to the left but when the Barbican diversion was completed all tracks continued straight on from the platforms.

The volume of traffic was severely down from pre-war levels. In 1959, only thirteen Eastern Region through trains arrived at Moorgate in the morning peak, and only ten departed in the evening peak. The London Midland Region services were even thinner, with merely two Moorgate arrivals in the morning peak and two departures in the evening. The LMR applied in 1965 for permission to withdraw all their Widened Lines passenger services, but permission was refused by the Minister of Transport. In 1967 BR put forward a more spectacular proposal – a medium-term scheme to close St Pancras completely and redevelop the site for offices. Midland multiple-unit electrics would run as far north as Leicester, with Moorgate as the London terminus. Traffic from north of Leicester would be diverted to Euston. At the same time, authority was sought to electrify the Great Northern suburban services and divert some trains to Moorgate via the Northern City Line, thereby abandoning the Great Northern services over the Widened Lines. The St Pancras closure was not approved. No immediate action was taken but the Widened Lines services could not escape the tide of diesel conversion which was sweeping steam traction away from the whole of BR. The Eastern Region services to Moorgate were converted to diesel operation on 23rd March 1959, and the London Midland from 21st September 1959 to 11th January 1960.

In 1970 the service on the City Widened Lines was in a run-down state, with freight traffic having been discontinued completely, and diesel multiple-units struggling through to Moorgate in Monday–Saturday peak hours only. The Eastern Region trains were the first to disappear, with the creation of an alternative through route from Finsbury Park to Moorgate via the erstwhile Northern City Line from 8th November 1976. The last train from Moorgate (CWL), one of the Saturday lunchtime workings, left on 6th November, though some scheduled trains did work through during the first months of 1977 to ease pressure during the reconstruction of King's Cross main line terminus. The last day of operation was 4th March 1977, after which the tunnels constituting the notorious York Road and Hotel Curves rested in peace.

In the London Midland Region, electrification of the Moorgate/St Pancras – Bedford line was authorised in 1977, and the Widened Lines and their approach tracks from Islip Street junction, near Kentish Town, were closed for electrification, the last diesel train being the 17.58 from Moorgate on 11th May 1979. Much work had to be done in track relaying (there was concrete slab track from Farringdon to Kentish Town), erecting overhead masts and wires, and resignalling, and in building a new street-level station at King's Cross. After some industrial relations and technical difficulties the first public passenger-carrying electric train ran to Moorgate on 11th July 1983, with the full passenger service coming into operation on 23rd January 1984. The Secretary of State for Transport unveiled a plaque in the newly-opened King's Cross (Midland City) ticket hall during the official opening on 15th July 1983.

The northern side of the Circle has witnessed some strange and largely unadvertised projections of Wimbledon or Putney Bridge to Edgware Road trains to Aldgate. For many years, probably beginning in 1945, these had run, at times of maximum traffic demand, on the Fridays before a bank holiday (Maundy Thursday for Easter and Christmas Eve for Christmas) and also on the bank holidays themselves. Days and timings varied from one year to the next, but a typical period of operation for pre-bank holiday projections was between 12.00 and 16.00, and on bank holidays themselves between 10.00 and the last train of the parallel services. This was altered to 22.00 in the last two years of operation (1968 and 1969). There is no record of bank holiday services after 1953 except for 1968/9. The last recorded pre-bank holiday service was in 1964.

Meanwhile, economy drives and the disappearance of Saturday peak traffic to the City of London resulted in the withdrawal of through 'peak' trains from the Metropolitan extension line to the City on Saturdays from October 1964 (Uxbridge and Watford trains) and October 1966 (the half-hourly Amersham trains). The Circle and Hammersmith & City trains now had to handle all the Saturday traffic between Edgware Road and Liverpool Street with a combined service of about 16 trains per hour. Observations of the Saturday afternoon traffic on this busy stretch indicated that something more was required, and from 19th October 1968, some trains from the Wimbledon branch to Edgware Road were projected to Moorgate, Liverpool Street or Aldgate stations from about 12.15 to 14.15, and again between 17.15 and 19.15. The projections, at about 15-minute intervals, were nearly all to Liverpool Street in the midday period and to Aldgate in the evening. It ran for the last time on 5th February 1972, although District crews continued to be trained to operate trains along this section (for many years four Sunday Circle Line trains were operated by the District for this purpose).

In 1960 the basic service was at 7½-minute intervals on Mondays to Saturdays (10 minutes evening) and 12 minutes on Sundays. In October 1967 the elimination of scheduled waits en route took precedence over recovering from running delays, and the 7½-minute basic service was increased to 7 minutes. However, the elimination of the scheduled waits had very adverse effects on maintaining the service, and a 7½-minute interval was resumed in January 1970. On 8th February 1970 the Sunday service was increased from every 12 to every 10 minutes, and the number of District trains allocated to the Circle on Sundays was increased from two to four. In November 1970 the peak hour service was reduced from 7½ to 8 minutes, allowing a total of 8 minutes recovery time on the complete circuit.

White City (Exhibition) station was abandoned on Sunday 25th October 1959 because of a destructive fire on the eastbound platform. It was not in any case regularly used and there were other stations nearby (it last seems to have been in use to handle Rugby crowds on 21st October).

Although not relevant to the operation of Circle Line trains themselves, it is worth noting that many stations on the south side of the Circle had not been long enough for the District Line's 7- or 8-car trains and in many cases narrow catwalks had been built into the tunnels so that passengers could get out of the doors at the extreme ends (though even then some doors had to be kept locked). This highly unsatisfactory arrangement resulted in a programme of expensive platform extension from 1955, which was where possible co-ordinated with general station renovation.

The then Charing Cross Underground station underwent several changes. The time-honoured exhibition space at the west end of the ticket hall fell victim to the need for space for automatic fare collection equipment, and the last occasion when it was used for public information was a seven-week run of a film about the Victoria Line in late 1969. The ticket offices were modernised and extended at the same time. Previously, some fairly extensive work had been done to cope with the expected heavy traffic to the main 1951 Festival of Britain site on the south bank of the Thames. The tube lines had two new escalators but for the District and Circle the improvements were confined to two new staircase-exits from near the east ends of the platforms. One debouched on to the Victoria Embankment, the other into Embankment Gardens. They were taken out of use after the end of the Festival, but have proved very effective in collecting dead leaves.

Sloane Square was another station where work was done in readiness for the expected heavy traffic flows to the Festival of Britain. The station was to be the railhead for a special bus service to the Festival of Britain fun-fair and pleasure gardens in Battersea Park. The brand new station of March 1940 had been open for less than eight months when it was destroyed by a bomb in November 1940. The replacement facilities had all been of a temporary character, including the ticket office, stairways and platform canopies. In the 1940 reconstruction the platforms had been lengthened 67ft at their western ends, and a steel raft built over the tracks. This was relatively undamaged by the bombing. The current reconstruction work was largely based on the pre-war plans, but there was an additional passenger exit in Holbein Place to relieve pressure in the main ticket hall. The rebuilt ticket hall incorporated the planned 1940 retail outlets in the shape of a tobacconist's, but the sites of a newsagents and a buffet were occupied by temporary supplementary ticket offices until the Festival was over. An 'up' escalator from each platform was reinstated, and the staff accommodation on the platforms was also restored. The street-level entrance and ticket hall were designed as a plinth for a later multi-storey block of offices. Some of the temporary construction was retained to give extra facilities for Festival traffic, ready for opening in May 1951. The proposed office development over the ticket hall began in late 1962 and was finished in late 1965 with seven storeys above ground level.

The modernised platforms at Charing Cross in 1951 (today's Embankment). Further modernisation here took place in 1988. LT Museum

The remains of the C.W. Clark station building at Notting Hill Gate in February 1957 in temporary use until the completion of the new subways provided a combined Central, District and Circle lines station. LT Museum

At Notting Hill Gate, separate stations for the Central and Metropolitan lines had existed since the tube line opened in 1900. A plan for a combined station had been prepared in the late 1930s, and some work had been done when the scheme was publicised in September 1938. The station scheme was an integral part of a road-widening plan. If the two Underground stations were demolished and replaced by a sub-surface ticket hall, the trunk A40 road could be widened, and the Underground passengers would benefit from low-level interchange between lines and escalators to the tube platforms. World War II brought work to a halt. The project lay dormant until March 1956, when progress was made possible by the London County Council's agreeing to pay part of the estimated £990,000 cost. The sub-surface ticket hall would be reached from five street stairways (one in Pembridge Gardens) and would also serve as a pedestrian subway. There would be three banks of escalators from the ticket hall to the lowest tube platform. The scheme was announced as the biggest Underground station reconstruction scheme since World War II ended, and the LT Annual Report for 1956 described it as an unfinished part of the 1935/1940 New Works Programme.

By August 1957 the C.W. Clark surface station had disappeared; a temporary ticket office and entrances had been installed in the previous March. The new ticket hall was to be in a reinforced-concrete 'box', capped by a roof of similar material. Part of it opened in August 1958 to serve the Circle Line passengers. The two street stairways on the south side of Notting Hill Gate opened at the same time.

For the passengers who travelled through the station on the Circle, there was little sign of change. The stairways down to the Central Line were the only visible new work, but the Circle was affected more profoundly than it appeared from the platforms. At the north end, building the sub-surface ticket hall had involved cutting away the original round-topped brick tunnel and substituting new side-walls and a steel-and-concrete raft for the floor of the ticket hall. Just south of this, 50ft of the Circle station walls had to be underpinned to allow the interchange subway to be built beneath. The full ticket hall opened on 1st March 1959, together with the new interchange subway and two banks of escalators.

Moorgate was crying out for extensive reconstruction after its wartime battering, but this had to await financial support from a property redevelopment scheme. A ten-stage scheme was devised, for £5 million-worth of office and shop development, including three 10-storey blocks and a first-floor shopping piazza above the station. The start of work on the development scheme on 8th December 1969 was widely publicised, and Stage 3 had been reached by September 1970. The work incorporated a new ticket hall and street entrance for the Metropolitan and Widened Lines.

The conversion of the Circle and Hammersmith & City fleets to 6-car trains of 'CP' and 'CO' types, by early 1963, made it possible to integrate the maintenance of this fleet at Hammersmith depot, with out-stationing at night (by rotation) at Neasden depot and the sidings at Aldersgate, Barking, Edgware Road and Farringdon. Neasden depot was thereby relieved of the duty of maintaining Circle stock.

By 1968 the 'CO' and 'CP' stock of 1937–1940 was beginning to show its age after years of intensive use, and London Transport was able to devise arguments that were persuasive enough for the Government to agree the purchase of 212 cars to replace all the existing rolling stock on the Circle and Hammersmith & City lines, i.e. thirty-five 6-car trains and two spare cars, divided between 17 trains for the Hammersmith & City timetable, and 14 for the Circle, and two cars to meet the requirements for engineers' spares. All the 212 cars of the order placed in May 1968 with Metropolitan-Cammell were to be made up into 2-car units, comprising one driving motor car and one trailer without a driver's cab. Each train would consist of three units. The individual units were not 'handed', so that they could still couple satisfactorily if an individual unit had been turned end-to-end, although there would, of course, have to be driving cabs at the ends of trains. In order to equalise the wear on the wheels on each side, a few trains were timetabled to be turned round by running Circle trains to depot via Aldgate East.

The first 'C69' train was delivered to Ruislip depot on 14th April 1970, transferred to Neasden for high-speed braking tests on 6th September 1970, and entered service on the Hammersmith & City on 28th September 1970. The first 'C69' train entered Circle line service on 8th February 1971, and the last arrived at Ruislip depot in September 1971.

The passenger saloons of the motor cars and trailers were of the same internal length, but the cabs of the motor cars were, in effect, added at one end, so that the motor cars measured 52ft 7in over body ends and the trailer cars 49ft 0in. The spacing of the bogie centres was increased by 4ft on the motor cars to keep down the length of the body overhang. Each car had four double doors on each side to allow for the Circle traffic characteristics of short passenger journeys between closely-spaced stations. Transverse double seats were provided between each pair of double doors, but there was one longitudinal seat for two passengers at each side of each car end, making a total of 32 seats in each car. Much standing space was provided, including that released by setting back the screens flanking the doorways. Car ventilation was provided by fixed openings above cantrail level (with a degree of adjustment for use by passengers) and also by roof-mounted heater-blowers, but, as has happened with other types of Underground stock, fans have proved unreliable in the testing environment of rapid-transit service.

With eventual one-person operation in mind, the door-control equipment was placed in each of the driving cabs. A new feature was a facility for selective door closing, allowing for all but one pair of doors in a car to be closed while the train was standing still awaiting a green signal, avoiding unnecessary heat loss in cold weather. The drivers'

'C' stock Circle working at Edgware Road. LT Museum

cabs had air-operated sliding doors (interlocked with the driver's control circuit) with inflatable air seals to keep out draughts. Lighting was by fluorescent tubes fed at 115 volts, 850 cycles from a motor-alternator unit and a transformer.

Television cameras and monitors were provided at Circle and Hammersmith & City stations in readiness for one-person operation, but this was not introduced for several years. Fourteen trailers were equipped with de-icing equipment, controllable from any driving cab.

When consideration was given to providing an entirely new fleet for the District, special attention had to be paid to the High Street Kensington–Edgware Road section, where the intermediate stations could not accommodate trains longer than six standard cars. The Wimbledon–Edgware Road service was therefore treated as an independent operation for which cars of the 'C69' type would be suitable. Eleven 6-car trains, designated 'C77' stock, were ordered from Metro-Cammell. This stock was designed to be operationally compatible with the 'C69' Stock, but incorporating a few detailed improvements. The first cars were delivered on 30th July 1977, put into service on the Hammersmith & City on 12th December 1977, and on to the Edgware Road–Wimbledon section on 17th April 1978.

London Underground Ltd

In 1984 London Transport passed once more to full government control and was restyled London Regional Transport (LRT). In pursuit of further devolution of authority, LRT was required to transfer its Underground responsibilities to a wholly-owned subsidiary company, London Underground Ltd, with effect from June 1985. There was no immediate change in day-to-day operation of the Hammersmith & City or Circle lines which continued to be operated by the Metropolitan & Jubilee division of the operating department, but from 1988 a new organisation was set up (the Hammersmith & Circle Line) which had full accountability for delivering day-to-day train services on both those lines, and later acquired full maintenance responsibilities. This was a factor in deciding to give the Hammersmith & City Line its own separate public identity, a change in the line colour to pink, from 30 July 1990. The management units re-merged in 1996 but separate identities were retained.

Cost savings had been the principal incentive for the management's wish to dispense with the services of guards on Underground trains. One-person operation (known as one-man operation in its early days) was proposed for the Circle and Hammersmith & City lines in 1972, but the concept was fiercely opposed by the trades unions representing operating grades, which fought a strong rearguard action. In 1973 it was announced that the Government and the GLC had agreed to contribute £1 million towards the gross costs of equipment to make these lines suitable for one-person operation. About 90 staff were expected to be saved.

After prolonged negotiations with the unions, London Transport introduced one-person operation on the Hammersmith & City Line on 26th March 1984, with four separate four-week periods of guards continuing to work on the trains, in three distinct roles. The management considered the experiment successful, and the practice continued, with the Circle Line being converted on 22nd October 1984. Subsequently, all other Underground lines were converted over an extended timescale.

After the King's Cross escalator fire of November 1987, in which 31 people perished, all the materials used in rolling stock were examined to see whether they presented similar risks to those which had been identified in stations. Although Underground rolling stock had always been built to high safety standards, some materials used in the stock could, in certain fire conditions, produce unacceptable toxic emissions, or discharge of melted material. These included melamine-faced hardboard and glass-reinforced plastic. Another fire risk was presented by leakage of the fluid in the parking brakes. Operational improvements included passenger alarms rather than direct passenger operation of the brakes, so that the train operator could decide whether to continue to the next station, where detrainment of passengers would be far easier than intermediately. Other refinements, which were fitted to new trains from the outset, included bright-beam headlights and automatic speed restriction after 'tripping' past a red signal.

Apart from safety issues, there was a need for both the interior and exterior of trains to present a neater, more attractive image. Repeated removals of graffiti had left the unpainted aluminium-alloy car exteriors in a poor state, and it was decided to revert to the previous practice of external painting, but with a special two-pack polyurethane system which was fire- and graffiti-resistant.

In 1989 one 2-car unit of mixed 'C69'/'C77' stock was sent to British Rail Engineering, Derby, for experimental refurbishment, and returned painted externally in the then-standard 'corporate' external livery of blue upper panels and white lower panels. Handrails finished in yellow replaced 'straps' for standing passengers. Each car had an experimental seating layout. In one, the transverse seats had been replaced by longitudinal, which entailed a loss of six seats per car. Fitting a shunting control cabinet in the end of a trailer gave a loss of another seat. Maple-wood flooring was replaced by the grooved, moulded type, and extra windows were fitted in the car ends for greater passenger security. A spring-loaded parking brake was substituted for hydraulic. Internally illuminated advertisement panels (never very successful) were removed. These two cars, in a train of four older cars, entered passenger service on 22nd November 1989.

The first 'production-run' train for refurbishment arrived at the premises of the successful contractor, RFS Industries, Doncaster, in July 1990. The standard livery now comprised grey roofs, red driving cabs and doors, white sides from below the roof to about a foot above the solebars, and dark blue for the lowest section. The car interiors, with new, near-white panelling, had a bright, spacious appearance, Seating capacity was retained at 32 per car, but all seats were longitudinal. New bogies were made, with the Metacone suspension replaced by rubber 'blobs', as on the District Line.

The final unrefurbished train left Ruislip depot for RFS Industries on 19th February 1994. It returned to passenger service on 5th May 1994. After refurbishment the trains were fitted with a system preventing the doors being opened on the wrong side at

'C' stock as refurbished between 1990 and 1994, seen at King's Cross St Pancras.

stations. Subsequently a 6-car train left Acton Works on 19th September 1997 after a digitised voice announcement system had been fitted, telling passengers the name of the next station or the name of the station at which the train was standing, and details of interchange lines. The system was subsequently fitted to all 'C69' group trains and identifies the train's location by the number of rotations of a trailer car axle.

The Circle Line does not lend itself to sweeping changes of frequency because of the constraints of the service interval having to divide exactly into the round running time (including scheduled pauses en route) and of having to interwork with parallel services notably the Hammersmith & City and District lines. However, a few notable improvements have been effected over the years.

We left the Circle in 1970 with an 8-minute weekday peak hour service and a 10-minute Sunday service. In May 1990 the Monday–Friday evening, Saturday and Sunday services were every 10 minutes. With the timetable change of that month, the practice of the District Line providing crews on Sundays was discontinued. This month also saw the projection of ex-Amersham and ex-Uxbridge trains from the Metropolitan extension line from Baker Street to Moorgate or Aldgate in the Monday–Friday midday and evening periods and all day on Saturdays and Sundays, considerably improving intervals on the north side of the Circle. In May 1994 the Monday–Friday midday and Saturday shopping period services became 8 minutes instead of 10 and the peak service to Barking was at 8-minute intervals instead of 16, following the completion of rolling stock refurbishment.

The most important change for the Hammersmith & City came on 29th September 1996, when alternate off-peak trains were extended from Whitechapel to Barking. This applied during the midday off-peak period and after the evening peak on Mondays to Fridays until 21.00. On Saturdays the extended service operated between 10.00 and 20.30. There was no corresponding change on Sundays, but the basic service was improved from a 10-minute to an 8-minute.

The Ladbroke Grove signal cabin was taken out of use after traffic on 12th March 1983 in readiness for the removal of the siding and crossover and conversion of the signals to standard two-aspect automatic. The unusual mechanical 15-lever frame was given to the National Railway Museum at York. The siding had seen its last regular use (on a Great Western steam shuttle service to Richmond) on 31st December 1910. The station name acquired the suffix 'For Portobello Road' from start of traffic on 9th April 1997.

The large signal box at Aldgate closed from 24th January 1988 and was replaced by modern interlocking machines controlled from a temporary panel in Farringdon box. In the period 1998-2001 the control of all semi-automatic signalling between Kings Cross and Aldgate was transferred to a new control centre at Baker Street with a computer switching trains automatically at Aldgate unless the control centre intervened. Farringdon signal box finally closed from 15th April 2001.

At Baker Street a new interlocking machine room was commissioned from 26th July 1987, although control was still exercised from the existing signal box through a temporary key-operated panel until 12th June 1988 when it was transferred to the new control centre.

As with orthodox surface buildings, tunnels and covered ways need regular inspection and constant maintenance. In 1976 work began on the brick tunnels whose interior surfaces had suffered the worst deterioration. Dirt and loose mortar were removed by high-pressure water jets and the remaining mortar raked out to a depth of at least half an inch. The joints between bricks were filled with mortar under high pressure from a pointing gun. The mortar was composed of cement, pulverised fuel ash and a chemical additive. In certain places where voids had been detected behind the inner bricks, holes were drilled to allow the insertion of pipes carrying pressurised liquid cement. In other cases, where water seepage was occurring, pipes were inserted through the full tunnel lining and a sand-cement mixture injected.

The covered way under Parliament Square has always been given special attention, doubtless with the thought in mind that any catastrophic collapse would be under the noses of the law-makers. Back in 1878, the District directors heard of a proposal to erect there the 180-ton, 68ft high stone obelisk known as Cleopatra's Needle, and asked to be indemnified against the risks of accident. It was erected on the Victoria Embankment instead. Earlier it was told how the roofs were strengthened in 1968 by fitting additional steel beams, or beams of pre-stressed concrete in the covered way on the St James's Park – Westminster section. Up to four new beams were erected in one night under Parliament Square. In 1996, an area was fenced off to prevent crowds gathering above the railway. In 1999, worries were expressed about the effect of large numbers of people congregating in the square to celebrate the arrival of New Year's Day 2000. Therefore a hidden load-bearing platform was inserted over the Circle and District lines in the middle of the square, without interruption to road or rail traffic.

Throughout this history there have been references to structural defects in the 'covered ways' needing urgent remedial work by civil engineers. One problem that made its presence known in the 1990s was just south of High Street Kensington station where there were two parallel double track covered ways, one for the Circle Line and one for the District's High Street – Earl's Court service. In 1993 the roof over the covered ways failed a safety test, and Kelso Place, Kensington was barred to vehicles weighing more than 13 tonnes. The two sections, built with cast iron girders and brick jack arches (both lying across the direction of the track) were little more than 100 metres long. but complicated and expensive structural surgery could not be delayed beyond 1999 on the Circle part. A further problem was that the headroom between the roofs and the tracks was less than the current standards. There were further problems in the shape of uncertainties about the stability of the brick retaining walls, and the discovery of major sewers close below the tracks.

The favoured solution was to make new steel beams of 'aerofoil' cross-section, to be installed tight up under the jack arches and supported on concrete-filled recesses in the vertical walls. There was room to make slight improvements to the headroom by excavating the trackbed. Each covered way needed 45 new beams, but five different versions were needed to cater for variations in the Victorian construction techniques. Engineers' possessions could have occupied one complete week, 28 consecutive week-end closures, as well as work every night. It was thought that complete closure for 9 weeks would cause less disturbance overall.

In April 1999 the high-powered London Underground publicity machine swung into action with leaflet deliveries to the local residents about the nine-week engineering works and line blockage, starting on 12th June and finishing on 15th August. There would be no service between Gloucester Road and High Street Kensington and a reduced service between the last-mentioned station and Edgware Road. Otherwise the Circle Line would be served by a modified service entering or leaving the loop at Earl's Court.

The modified service involved the Edgware Road – Wimbledon service, the main District Line service to Wimbledon, and the Kensington Olympia service. The District trains were removed from the Olympia service, also between Earl's Court and

Wimbledon except in the Monday to Friday peaks. Because the Olympia branch could not reverse an 8-minute service the scheduled service was 'lopsided'. Trains leaving Wimbledon every 8 minutes made a complete circuit of the inner rail Circle and returned to Wimbledon. However, another group left every 16 minutes and should have been joined at Earl's Court by another 16-minute service from Olympia. The joint 8-minute service would traverse the outer rail circle, and continue to Earl's Court for Olympia and Wimbledon alternately. Thus, passengers from the Wimbledon line wishing to make the popular journey to High Street Kensington or Bayswater had only a 16-minute direct through service, although they had an 8-minute service on their return. If this had been a schedule for a model railway with no passengers or staff, and impeccable reliability, it might have worked very well and earned the compiler a medal for his ingenuity. In the real world it had to contend with the usual ration of equipment breakdowns, unsatisfactory crew relief arrangements, insufficient turnaround time at termini, and passengers delaying trains at stations until they were sure where the trains were going. Also, too many trains were scheduled through Earl's Court in the peaks (38 in one hour of the morning peak compared with the usual 34).

As soon as the service was due to run, it was delayed by early morning power problems, followed by crew relief problems. The service was in chaos by 14.00 and the only remedy was to split the workings into self-contained sections. An afternoon points failure caused a 20-minute suspension. The first working day (Monday 14th June) began with a 2-hour 40-minute signal failure causing suspension between High Street Kensington and Edgware Road. By late morning the scheduled services were abandoned and extempore self-contained services run for the rest of the day. Finally it was announced that the special service would be abandoned from Monday 21st June. The Circle service would be withdrawn completely and the District service revert to its normal timetable. The Hammersmith & City Line had been little changed under the special timetable, but some extra trains were employed to shuttle between Hammersmith and Aldgate in the peaks and between Edgware Road and Plaistow in the off-peak. From 5th July two 'C' stock trains were allocated to Ealing Common depot to relieve the central section of the District Line, by shuttling between Putney Bridge and Mansion House. This was the first-ever allocation of 'C' stock to Ealing Common.

The work was due to be completed by 16th August, but flooding and a burst sewer caused a one-week delay. Services did not resume until 23rd August with the new anti-vibration ballast matting being in place on the affected section. However, the 44 'aerofoil' roof beams were not all in place by the delayed opening date 'owing to logistical problems', although the covered way was safe because the cast-iron roof beams had been reinforced with carbon-fibre plastic plates. The remaining new beams would have to be inserted in normal engineering hours.

When the problem of the two covered ways had first been announced, it was stated that the one in the western arm of the Cromwell triangle would be tackled in summer 2000 so that the Earl's Court–High Street Kensington trains (and those in the opposite direction) would reverse in Gloucester Road station. By early summer 2000, nothing further had been heard of this project, but in September 2000 a Draconian plan was announced. In the peaks the Ealing and Richmond services would be halved, and the Olympia service withdrawn at all times. The Wimbledon–Edgware Road service would be diverted to Tower Hill, with passengers wishing to travel to High Street Kensington and points north having to change to the Circle at Gloucester Road. The plan was due to begin early in February 2001 and to operate for 3½ months. In practice work started

Bayswater station following reconstruction of the entrance and staircase.
Capital Transport

on 3rd February, and was completed on 18th May, with new working timetables due to start on Sunday 20th May. Unfortunately, engineering works concerned with points at Baker Street caused the suspension of all services by surface stock trains across the junction. This threw all 'C69' services into confusion throughout that weekend and it was not until 0800 on 21st May that more-or-less normal services were restored.

Under London Underground management, stations on the Hammersmith & City and Circle lines continued to be improved as and when funds permitted. Even so the observant eye may still detect signs of their Victorian origins and at some stations some effort has been made to restore Victorian features either hidden for many years, or badly disfigured by inappropriate past modernisation or simply by the ravages of time.

At Gloucester Road, High Street Kensington, Notting Hill Gate, Bayswater, Paddington (Circle), Baker Street (Circle), Great Portland Street, Euston Square Farringdon and Barbican, hoardings have been removed to uncover original Victorian brickwork which has been restored, together with new signs and improved lighting. Paddington also benefited from major works to update the Bakerloo station and this included an enlarged and remodelled ticket hall under the main line station during 1984-87 (further enlarged in 1999). The yellow brick retaining walls on the Circle were restored in 1986, as was the glazed overall roof and the iron lattice footbridge.

At Bayswater there was in 1996 a major reconstruction scheme. This was designed to relieve congestion at peak periods, when slow-moving tourists aroused the ire of would-be fast-moving commuters. The station closed on 22nd January 1996, and when it reopened on 18th March of that year it had been largely transformed. It had a new, wider footbridge across the tracks, two additional staircases, a wider street entrance with longer canopy and additional ticket gates.

Platform 4 at High Street Kensington had only one narrow staircase access and to ease congestion it was thought helpful to add a new platform-level walkway (around the back of the buffers) which linked it to platforms 2 and 3; this was opened on 22nd March 1993. To achieve this, platforms 3 and 4 had to be extended southwards by about 45 feet. The shopping arcade was enlarged and completely restyled in 1981 and 1987, providing one of the most attractive and stylish shopping malls in London.

At Tower Hill, the narrow booking hall opened in 1967 soon proved inadequate for the burgeoning tourist traffic, and it was demoted to being solely an exit on 20th November 1988, when a complete new sub-surface ticket hall was opened further west, reached by a short flight of steps. The area round the entrance was later landscaped.

At Gloucester Road, property development over the Circle and District stations funded the complete redecoration of the platforms and a new combined ticket hall at street level, at the expense of depriving the platforms of daylight, by erecting a concrete raft over all tracks and platforms. The development comprised shopping arcades with offices and luxury flats above. The platforms had their brick walls thoroughly cleaned and were illuminated by large pendant light fittings resembling the designs of 1868. Concealed lights behind the advertisement panels completed the bright effect. A large translucent-roofed ticket hall gave direct access to the surface line stairways and the Piccadilly lifts. The scheme was completed in June 1993.

A transformation of Monument station began with preparations for new escalators connecting with the Docklands Light Railway station at Bank, opened in 29th July 1991. These debouched in the Circle/District westbound platform. The new escalator concourse, and the existing ticket hall, were extensively modernised with grey wall tiles and grey terrazzo floors, with concealed lighting in the ceiling cornices and triangular uplighters on the pillars. The remainder of both platforms was subsequently redecorated in the same grey and polished stainless steel motif. The platforms walls sported bas-reliefs of dragons, one of the City of London's heraldic beasts.

Mansion House was closed for modernisation from 30th October 1989 to 10th February 1991, inclusive, in connection with redevelopment of the property above. The rebuilt station had a larger ticket hall and was finished with white wall tiles and mottled brown terrazzo flooring. New lights and signs completed the transformation of the station.

Westminster proved to be the most challenging project on the whole Jubilee Line extension from Green Park to Stratford. The new parliamentary building, Portcullis House, was built above the Circle/District station, which called for the tracks to be lowered by about 300mm to improve the headroom beneath its supports. This involved several weekend line closures, and transferring the existing tracks to a temporary bridge. The appearance of the Circle platforms was transformed by having to accommodate the upper landings of escalators down to an intermediate level. On the westbound platform a glass screen round the escalators was slightly obstructive to Circle/District passengers. After frantic efforts to finish the whole late-running extension by New Year's Eve 1999, the new Jubilee station (and its lift and escalator connections) was opened in the afternoon of 22nd December 1999 by which date the Circle Line's new platforms were in use also.

The complete reconstruction of Liverpool Street main line terminus incorporated a large new ticket hall for the Circle and Central lines. Sited a few steps down from the main concourse, it is one of the largest on the Underground, and incorporates an 'egg-crate' false ceiling, white wall tiles and terrazzo flooring. It was completed in 1992.

The shopping arcade adjoining the original Metropolitan station in Liverpool Street was badly damaged by the Bishopsgate bomb of 1993, but was handsomely restored by April 1994, with 24 virtually-new shop units.

Hammersmith was noteworthy for the pioneer installation, in April 1987, of two new types of self-service ticket machine, as part of the comprehensive Underground Ticketing System. One issued tickets to ten destinations, the other, which was fully operational by the end of 1988, to all stations to which there were through bookings.

At the remote Latimer Road, modern station signs and fluorescent lighting were installed in February 1983. A major renovation of the ticket hall needed a two-day closure in 1985. In May 1998 work began to stabilise the railway embankment, but bird-lovers protested that the tree-clearance would threaten nesting birds. London Transport promised that any felled trees would be replaced. The eastbound platform was closed for reconstruction from 6th March 1999. Passengers from the Hammersmith direction wishing to alight there had to continue to Westbourne Park and return on the next westbound train. The work was completed on 28th March 1999, allowing similar work to start on the westbound platform on 10th April 1999, lasting until 1st May 1999. These works were publicised as a measure to allow passengers step-free access to and from trains.

Until the building of the Jubilee Line extension in the late 1990s, Westminster was one of just a few stations on the south side of the Circle Line that had not been modernised since World War II. The impressive new platforms came into use in 1999.
Capital Transport

On 12th February 1998 a 6-car train of 'C' Stock was unveiled to the press at High Street Kensington. It was in overall advertising livery to promote the Yellow Pages directories of trade suppliers. New moquette was fitted throughout, incorporating patterns of either the Yellow Pages logo or the names of services that could be contacted. The train ran in this condition for just over a year. Capital Transport

Crime at Shepherd's Bush Market had become a serious problem, and it was also experienced on the railway itself. A security control room was established in a spare room at Ladbroke Grove station with work starting at the end of summer 1987. The room contained colour television monitors which relayed images from each station on the line from Hammersmith to Paddington inclusive. The control room was in radio contact with staff at these stations, which were equipped with passenger alarm panels. There were telephone lines to the British Transport Police and to the Line Controller. The opportunities for crime were reduced by better lighting in dark corners, and mirrors in subways and corridors. The work was due for completion by May 2000.

Westbourne Park station was in the 'V' of the junction between the Hammersmith & City and the Great Western main line from Paddington to Slough and points west. The Hammersmith & City part of the station had been opened on 1st February 1866, followed by the main line part on 31st October 1871. Here it was a case of 'last in, first out' and the main line station closed on 14th March 1992, with demolition starting immediately so that the main line tracks could be realigned. However £½ million was spent on a safety upgrade in readiness for the 1995 Notting Hill carnival and special staffing and exit arrangements were made for succeeding carnivals.

The construction of a Channel Tunnel Rail Link to terminate at St Pancras threatened to overload the Underground facilities at King's Cross/St Pancras with passengers wishing to continue their journeys into central London. A large-scale enlargement scheme for the Underground station began in June 2001.

Whither the Circle?

As a footnote to any book about the Circle Line ought to be mentioned the constant background pressure from within the organisation to abandon a style of train service which is extremely awkward to operate and whose consequent unreliability fails to serve the travelling customer as well as it might. We have already seen that London Transport had, in 1934, successfully sought to have the statutory obligation to run the service removed; the problem was that it was popular and reasonable alternatives appeared expensive.

The Circle Line has probably always been unreliable, for the reasons enumerated earlier, and electrification only improved affairs to a degree. By 1919 even Frank Pick had become disenchanted with it and observed that only 20 per cent of users of Circle Line trains used its unique 'round the corner' sections and that in consequence even more valuable paths along the northern and southern sections were inefficiently occupied and were better used by Metropolitan or District trains. He proposed breaking the western curve between Gloucester Road and High Street Kensington and sending the District's Putney–High Street Kensington trains alternately to the District main line and the Metropolitan in paths released by Circle trains as a more useful contribution. Although this was not pursued at the time (and may then have been precluded by statute) the Circle Line problem festered on as a not wholly satisfactory service looking for an acceptable solution.

Many suggestions have been made as to how to address the issue. In 1948 the idea was floated of running a Circle-and-a-half by having trains leave Putney Bridge for Edgware Road, then complete one orbit of the Circle and continue beyond Edgware Road and Baker Street to terminate at King's Cross. In terms of trains-per-hour over sections, this was equivalent to projecting the Putney Bridge–Edgware Road trains to King's Cross. It would have involved working 40 trains per hour over the Baker Street flat junction and on to King's Cross. In 1950, consideration of the idea was deferred because of the then-current proposal to send the southern end of the Victoria Line to Fulham Broadway, with trains continuing to Wimbledon. If this had happened, the Circle-and-a-half would have run between Fulham Broadway and Baker Street. Detailed studies showed that it would have required two new reversing roads at Baker Street from the west, which would have been prohibitively expensive.

Therefore the proposal for a Circle-and-a-half terminating at King's Cross was revived in April 1951. At that time the Putney Bridge–Edgware Road trains were of 6-car length, and the Circles 5-car. Although the Circle trains were, in fact lengthened to 6-car in 1959/60, the cost of 14 extra cars to achieve 6-car Circles was debited to the project, together with a further six cars for one extra train. With the added costs of civil engineering and signalling work at King's Cross, the estimated project total became £422,000. The economic climate of the time (1952) favoured reduction of off-peak car mileage, not an increase, and the scheme petered out.

In 1949 an internal London Transport memorandum suggested taking advantage of bombed areas in the City of London by diverting the District Line via Fenchurch Street station, and building two extra (parallel) tracks between Aldgate and Monument for Circle trains which would terminate from the east at a rebuilt two-island Monument station. Passengers from west of Monument to Liverpool Street could use the new tubes planned in May 1949 (or take a District train and change at Monument). Proposals for the western end of the truncated Circle were not specified but this section could have terminated in the South Kensington central bay road planned in the Gloucester Road scheme, resulting in a South Kensington–Monument shuttle.

A later idea, of 1984, was designed to find a use for the unloved 1983 tube stock and to allow London Transport to compete for traffic from the Circle Line area to Heathrow Airport. (Heathrow Express from Paddington had been approved in the previous year). One group of trains would have left Heathrow (Piccadilly) at 15-minute intervals, moved on to the District at Hammersmith, and from High Street Kensington proceeded round the Circle outer rail to continue to Earl's Court, Hammersmith and the Piccadilly Line. A second group would have left Heathrow at 15-minute intervals and followed the same route as the first except that it would proceed direct from Earl's Court to Gloucester Road and continue anti-clockwise round the Circle, then as the first route reversed. Half the existing Circle service would have continued to run. This proposals was quickly abandoned because of unattractive frequencies and the problem of squeezing extra trains through Earl's Court. A rump of this idea persisted in a scheme to use the 1983 stock on a High Street Kensington – Hammersmith – Uxbridge service, allowing all the main Piccadilly trains to run to Heathrow. This scheme soon died, and the earlier batch of the 1983 Stock was scrapped.

In the next stage, some ideas of how to eliminate the Circle were tried out in practice. The annual Notting Hill Carnival was held at the end of August, and attracted steadily increasing traffic. For the Sundays and Mondays of the August Bank Holiday weekend of 1990, 1991 and 1992, the Hammersmith & City was amalgamated with the Circle Line, so that, for example, a train would leave Hammersmith and continue by the normal route to Liverpool Street, whence it would take the Circle route. After arriving at Liverpool Street a second time, it would resume its original route to Whitechapel, where it would terminate. A similar working applied in the opposite direction. In the first year hints were dropped that this might become a standard daily operation, if the experiment was successful, but after 1992 it was concluded that the scheme was confusing to passengers and difficult to operate, since it was very difficult to restore regular running after any major delays – despite the fact that the main object of the scheme was to provide some recovery time in the timetable. Subsequent official pronouncements hinted that the scheme might be revived, but no more was heard of it.

Finally we have Mr Derek Smith, then Managing Director of London Underground, addressing the London Regional Passengers Committee on 24th November 1999 – 'The Circle Line's contribution to the totality of the network is not large, and it makes control of the shared lines difficult. It is not the right design, and in the long term the question is whether it should continue'.